The Gold-Plated PORSCHE

The Gold-Plated
PORSCHE

How I Sank a Small Fortune into a
Used Car, And Other Misadventures

STEPHAN WILKINSON

The Lyons Press
Guilford, Connecticut
An imprint of The Globe Pequot Press

For The Girls

The Lyons Press is an imprint of The Globe Pequot Press

10   9   8   7   6   5   4   3   2   1

Printed in the United States of America

Designed by Christine Mongillo

Portions of Chapters 9, 18, and 35 appeared in a slightly different form in *Popular Science Magazine.*

ISBN 1-59228-256-3

Library of Congress Cataloging-in-Publication Data is available on file.

CONTENTS

PREFACE

I do love to take things apart and put them back together again. My favorite toy as a child, way back in the early 1940s, was an Erector Set. The metal kind, with tiny but real nuts and bolts. No snap-lock fittings or Velcro or E-Z fasteners, just hundreds of little square nuts, and bolts of various lengths. I can still see them in my memory, as well as the tiny wrench and screwdriver that tightened them. I can see the shiny sheet-metal girders with their cross-hatching of stiffeners, the bright-colored gears, the wheels (red centers, chrome rims), the minute-set screws that locked them to shafts that powered little Ferris wheels, mock airplane propellers, carts and wagons, and Rube Goldberg devices that delighted simply by moving. You built something, took it apart, and then built something else. If only life were so easy.

The biggest Erector Set, the 100-pound Model 10, included plans for a four-foot-long locomotive and an even bigger Zeppelin. Come to think of it, real Zeppelins looked as though they'd been made from life-size Erector Sets.

An electric motor about the size of a sewing-machine motor—big, by toy standards—powered the things. It's probably one reason why Erector Sets no longer exist. You actually *plugged it into a wall socket,* thus risking electrocution if, say, you decided to lick the motor, drop it into the toilet, or stick your little screwdriver into the socket instead. No puny batteries included.

Don't get me started, but one of the reasons so many of my friends and acquaintances are amazed that I took apart and put back together again a 1983 Porsche 911SC sports car of considerable complexity is that they never had Erector Sets. They weren't allowed to electrocute themselves, or spear a slipped screwdriver through a finger, or wrap their little brother's hair so tightly into the gears and cogs of a windup toy train that he had to be cut loose. (Sorry, Kirk. That *was* dumb of me.)

They became adults during a time of increasing government benevolence, of officialdom protecting us against ourselves at the behest of coteries of hysterics demanding total, I-can't-be-responsible-for-myself safety.

My wife some time ago discovered the secret of getting out of jury duty. Not that she wanted to avoid her civic duty, but the lawyer for the plaintiff—the suit involved a drunk who had slipped on the ice and fractured her hip while leaving a local saloon—asked during jury-selection how Susan felt about personal-liability litigation.

"Hey, life's a risk," Susan said.

"OUT," the lawyer said.

Someday, we won't even be allowed to take apart our cars, much less modify their engines—as I did—with wild camshafts, archaic carburetors, exhaust systems fat as Foster's beer cans, and ignition systems powerful enough to fry Frankenstein. What am I talking about? In some states, this is *already* illegal.

But I'd always wanted to take a car apart—*really* apart—and put it back together again. Of course, you put it back together as good as new, maybe better, and this is what collectors call a frame-off restoration: everything comes off the frame, gets restored, and then gets reassembled. You become a one-person car factory, doing all over again what the manufacturer did years ago.

I got a variety of reactions to my declaration that I was going to restore an '83 Porsche 911 and do it all myself. "For the money you're going to spend, you could simply buy a late-model Turbo," said one well-meaning adviser. "Instant horsepower."

Exactly. It would cost me $70,000 and an hour of signing papers at a Porsche dealership, and I'd be done. What's the fun in that?

"I have little idea what's under the hood and less interest in how it works," said a talented racer friend. "I want to race the car, not work on it."

Well, even Formula 1 world champion Michael Schumacher as a teenager worked at a Mercedes-Benz dealership in Germany, servicing sedans. I'm sure *he* knows what's under the hood.

Finally, I took to explaining that I was simply spending two years and $70,000 to make a brand-new 1983 Porsche that would never in my lifetime be worth more than twenty grand, tops. It was like the Master-Card commercials: "Car, $10,500. Parts, $59,500. Experience, priceless." A few people got it, most didn't. This book is for the people who Get It.

Chapter One

GETTING UPSIDE-DOWN

My butt was in the seat, and my key was in the ignition— the classic left-of-the-wheel ignition tumbler of a Porsche. My Porsche. My totally restored, outrageously upgraded, I-did-it-all-myself, who-cares-what-it-cost 1983 911SC Coupe. My inexplicable demonstration of the fact that it's entirely possible to spend two years and $69,805.55 remanufacturing an archaic, iconic, but not particularly rare high-performance car to create something worth far less than the sum of its parts. Investment-minded classic-car collectors call it "getting upside-down."

And now it was time to put to the test the very tender portion of it upon which I'd alone spent about $15,000 on special German Mahle pistons, cylinder barrels, and rings; valves, springs, and trick Aase titanium followers; rods, bearings, and worth-their-weight ARP studs and fasteners; brand-new timing chains, sprockets, and cam tensioners; ported, polished, and laboriously bench-flowed twin-plug cylinder heads; two expensive PMO triple-barrel carburetors; and freshly re-profiled camshafts.

It was time to test the engine.

I had totally disassembled it, cleaned and polished every part that wasn't replaced with a new one, and then rebuilt the thing—very carefully, very slowly, very nervously. You see, I had never before been inside a Porsche engine, and there were many knowledgeable gear-heads who'd said rebuilding a 911 engine in an amateur's workshop, with an amateur's hands and tools, was akin to doing neurosurgery on the kitchen table.

Would it start? Would it detonate? Melt? Seize? Run backward? (A possibility, believe it or not.) Had I bolted everything together just right? Tightened and torqued perfectly, sealed and gasketed correctly, timed the valves so they wouldn't clap hands with the pistons? My lack of confidence was evident: with the car sitting in a 150-year-old tinder box of a wooden barn, I had carefully positioned behind the car a five-gallon Spackle bucket filled with water, ready to put out the blaze. (My lack of common sense was also evident: water would only spread a gasoline fire, not drench it.)

As I sat in the driver's seat, I mused briefly about that unusual left-handed ignition-key location. Unusual enough that even 911 owners, who typically have numerous other cars in their garages as well, sometimes find themselves fumbling for a key with the same right hand they use in their Mercedes sedan or Lexus SUV.

Legend has it that Porsche to this day retains the anomaly because it dates back half a century to the time when the factory first contested Le Mans, a race it was eventually to win outright sixteen times. In the sporty 1950s, drivers actually made what came to be called "Le Mans starts." They would stand across the wide racetrack from their cars, diagonally parked nose-out in a long row, fastest cars at the front, and sprint to them when the flag dropped. (Well, the young bulls sprinted; the more portly gentleman racers trotted.) The drivers would vault in, fire the engine, put the car in gear and go, and how quickly the engine started and the car got into gear and away was part of the game.

A silly part, since the race was twenty-four hours long, and ten minutes one way or the other rarely made a difference. It really didn't matter if you ran to the car like Carl Lewis or wandered across the track like somebody looking for his Ford Explorer in a mall parking lot. Other than that, too much wandering would eventually leave you in the middle of a swarm of fast-moving traffic.

Porsche, coolly logical Germans that they were, figured that putting the key on the left would allow the driver to crank the starter with the left hand while putting the shifter into first with the right, saving a second or two.

But never mind. I was both wasting time and avoiding the inevitable.

"Ready?" I leaned out the door and hesitantly asked my friend Jim. Jim Catalano is an Adirondacker, a North Woodsman with the survival skills of a bull walrus. He has taught himself to do everything from automotive bodywork to fine-arts printmaking, from aircraft maintenance to welding, and it is to him that I go whenever I have a *practical* problem. Catalano at that moment had the fuselage of a 1930s Canadian Fleet biplane in his garage, undergoing a meticulous restoration, and in a small shed halfway down his rutted little rural driveway sat the Lotus Elan S2 that he has owned since the 1960s.

Catalano said, "Go for it."

I twisted the key and the starter whirred into life, for the first time in the almost two years since I'd first driven the little red—then—911SC off the flatbed delivery truck and up the driveway to our Upstate New York house. As two fat Blaster capacitor coils fed by a pair of MSD High-Energy Ignition units spritzed great shots of voltage to the twelve spark plugs, the engine . . .

Well, let's back up and start from the beginning.

Chapter Two

THE CHRISTMAS PRESENT

My carefully wrapped Christmas present that year was a $4.95 issue of *Hemmings Motor News,* the thick, pulp-paper monthly classified listing of collector cars. Even if it carries a twenty-first-century date, each issue still looks like something you'd find on the toilet tank of a 1950s Sinclair station restroom in Tucumcari, New Mexico. So was this a cheesy gift from my wife? Hardly.

"You look bored," Susan laughed at my bafflement. "You finished the addition to our house. You built an airplane. You're playing around with models."(No, no—the 1:48-scale plastic-kit kind, not the double-breasted variety.) "You need another project," she said.

"Buy yourself a car to restore. A Ferrari. An Aston Martin like the one you had when you were a young stud. A Corvette, a Cobra . . ."

Wow. I'd always wanted to restore a car, and my unfailingly perceptive partner, always game for anything, was encouraging me to start at the top. Husbands who feel that permission to watch the Super Bowl is marital bliss don't know what they're missing.

But I didn't want to get in over my head with an exotic car that required expensive specialist help. A hard-core anal compulsive, I'd always wanted to do that frame-off rebuild, totally disassembling a car, detailing every part, and reassembling it to . . . well, maybe not perfection, in this era of spare-no-expense professional automobile restorations worth more than Monets, but at least reassembled to sanitary standards.

I was casually contemptuous of collectors who claimed to have "restored" a car when in fact all they did was write checks. Anybody can do that. I wanted to do this car all by myself—engine, body, paint, interior, leather, electrical wiring, greasy bits, and all.

I also wanted a car that would provide a reasonable level of performance when I was done, not a 1950s classic that might have run strongly in fond memory—an XK-120, an MG TD, a Morgan—yet would make me turn to my wheezy old Saab whenever I felt the need to exceed the national speed limit. So the choice was easy, particularly with my then-nineteen-year-old car-enthusiast daughter, a Skip Barber graduate, chanting, "POR-shuh, POR-shuh, POR-shuh" in the background. I would seek out a restorable Porsche 911.

I still remember the awe I felt when I worked at *Car and Driver* magazine and was invited to visit the Porsche factory in Stuttgart in the mid-1970s, when Porsche 911s were still very special. The intensity of the hand-building process, the care and compulsion with which these little supercars were being assembled made me lust for one. It was a time when Porsche was segueing from being a maker of sparse, bare-bones enthusiast cars to being a manufacturer of what would soon be inordinately desirable luxury playthings, far too many of them newly bought by people who thought the name was pronounced "Porsh."

The legacy endures. In the 1980s the joke went, "What's the difference between a Porsche and a porcupine? In the case of a porcupine, the prick is on the outside." And more recently, an article in *Vanity Fair* recounted the rounds of a sex therapist who ministered to newly minted Los Angeles trophy wives. The women weren't sure how to administer the one thing all of their rich husbands most wanted—oral sex—so she gave group lessons using dildos of different sizes. The smallest rubber practice penis in her stock of toys was labeled, "the Porsche Driver."

In the '80s, Porsche 911s had become cars that you bought because you wanted to make plain your wealth and sophistication—cars that you acquired to demonstrate the fact that you could afford the best and were man enough to drive it. (An enormous percentage of 911 buyers were, and still are, male.)

Oddly enough, Porsche had planned to discontinue the 911 in the mid-1980s, which would have been a dreadful mistake. Management had decided that their two conventional front-engine, water-cooled models—the four-cylinder 924/944 and the V8 928—could join hands over the gap that would be created by dropping the air-cooled six, and that would carry the company into the future. All serious 911 development work had stopped in the late '70s.

With the unlikely accession of an American, Peter Schutz, to the chairmanship of Porsche in 1980, the 911 suddenly found itself back on the front burner. Schutz understood that the 911 was Porsche's rightful heritage and fertile future. An enthusiastic private pilot, he even had the company develop an aircraft version of the 911 engine. That was an expensive mistake, in part because the Germans figured they knew everything there was to know about air-cooled engines and refused to listen to any advice about cooling drag from the American aircraft manufacturer, Mooney, into whose airframes the engines were the first to be fitted.

As a result, the jewel-like 911 airplane engine never produced the airspeed cranked out by the crude, considerably cheaper air-cooled flat sixes and even four-cylinders made by the American manufacturers Lycoming and Continental, the latter of which at one time also made lumpish engines for Checker taxicabs.

I flew a Porsche powered Mooney once, in 1988, to write a "pilot report" (the aerial equivalent of a road test) for the English aviation magazine *Pilot,* and it was a splendid machine. Incredibly smooth, since the high-revving, overhead-camshaft German engine offered 1980s technology while the competing pushrod Lycoming four was essentially a product of the 1930s.

The Porsche engine was also operated like a jet, with a single "power lever" that controlled the throttle, the pitch of the propeller blades, and the mixture. "Mixture" is what you call the proportion of gasoline to air that flows into an engine's combustion chambers, since less and less gas is needed as an airplane climbs into thinner air at altitude. In all other piston-engine airplanes, a forest of throttle, prop, and mixture-control levers sprouts from the cockpit console and must constantly be tuned and adjusted like the stops on an organ.

Fine. But these niceties raised the price of the basic then-$150,000 Mooney by another $50,000. "For the price of a [Porsche-engine] Mooney," I wrote at the time, "you could buy a 160-knot Mooney 201 [with an American engine] plus a 165-mph Porsche 928 S4 automobile *and* have enough change left over to feed and maintain them both for a year." Soon thereafter, Mooney dropped its plans to offer the Porsche engine as an option.

Unfortunately, Schutz's booming Porsche automotive programs had already collided head-on with the stock-market crash of October 1987, when "Porsh" buyers suddenly found themselves downsizing to Jeep Cherokees. Nor did it help that Porsche had been over-reliant on the U.S. market, which bought almost two-thirds of all its cars, during a period when a very favorable exchange rate earned Porsche far more money than it normally would have made. But the value of the dollar had plummeted at the end of 1986. Schutz was forced out by Porsche's supervisory board in December, 1987 and replaced by a bean-counter, the company's finance director, Heinz Branitzki.

By 1992, Porsche production was down to 15,000 cars, little more than a quarter of the number they'd made in '86. But by that time, an enlightened new all-German management team was in place, after five years of post-Schutz floundering, and they made two major moves: They discontinued the excellent but conventional front-engine quasi-sports Porsches in favor of concentrating totally upon 911s and a remarkably successful new line of flat-six cars to be called Boxsters. And they hired Japanese production consultants to teach them how to manufacture superb sports cars without all that handwork and fussiness that had so impressed me when I visited the factory as a novice automotive journalist.

For decades, Porsche and Mercedes, particularly, boasted of how many of their new cars went straight from the assembly line to the fix-the-mistakes parking lot, to which they had been sent by picky quality-control inspectors who found paint scratches, skewed door hinges, too-wide panel gaps, and the like. There, rubber mallets became the tools of choice as workers pounded and persuaded misaligned metal back into shape, and these manufacturers even made a point of advertising their finickiness.

The Japanese were baffled. Why on earth let a car continue down the assembly line if it had a fault? What had created the fault in the first place? Stop the line and fix *that,* whether it was a workstation tool cart too close to a newly painted fender, a careless worker misusing an air wrench, or a slightly out-of-whack jig allowing hinges to be set improperly. Toyota didn't even *have* a fix-the-boogers parking lot.

Chapter Three

IN PURSUIT OF PURITY

Nine-elevens were never easy to drive, in large part because their handling peculiarities and simple but quirky rear-suspension design required drivers to do counterintuitive things, like not lifting off the throttle if they found themselves rounding a corner too fast. Not lift? How else do you slow down? Unfortunately, in a 911, you're pretty much committed to a high-speed corner at whatever your entry speed might have been.

A large percentage of a 911's weight is in its tail. While rounding a corner, that weight wants to swing like a pendulum toward the outside of the turn—to "oversteer," pulling the car into a spin. What prevents this is the grip of the rear tires, and holding a steady speed and throttle setting through the corner tends to maintain that grip because the car is "in balance," settled into its cornering posture and providing the maximum amount of weight and down force over the rear tires. (You could provide more down force by accelerating, causing the car to imperceptibly rear back over the drive wheels under the torquing force of the drive axles, but that would be a maneuver *so* counterintuitive that if you could do it, you're a race car driver and wouldn't be reading this anyway.)

OK, so you can't accelerate because you're already going too fast. What to do? Well, as the adrenaline heats your body like a flash of microwaves and every sensible input tells you to *brakebrakebrake,* stay on the gas just as you have been—no more, no less. You may still go off the road—there *are* physical inevitabilities—but at least it'll be a relatively controlled slide into the weeds, and you just might manage to squeak past disaster at the last minute.

The hell with it, you say, I'm not stupid enough to speed *into* an accident, I'm going to at least take my foot off the gas, probably even tap the brakes to slow down.

Instant 911 spin.

Charlotte Hornets basketball player Bobby Phills made the news in January of 2000 when he was killed in his new, very fast 911 convertible. He had apparently been running at over 100 mph alongside a teammate in another Porsche—who's to say whether they were racing or just driving fast?—on a long, sweeping bend on a four-lane undivided highway. "Somehow," as the TV commentators put it, his Porsche ended up sideways in the opposite-direction traffic lanes, and he was T-boned by an oncoming Buick.

The "somehow" was evident to every knowledgeable Porsche driver who watched the nightly news. It was the classic Porsche crash. Phills, perhaps newly wealthy enough to buy his first Porsche, had probably never driven one before. Good at hoops doesn't translate into cool hands on the road, but it's hard for a high achiever on a basketball court to accept the fact that he needs driver's ed on a fast road.

He went into the bend way too hot and almost certainly instinctively lifted off the throttle when he realized it. That's what he would have done in a Camaro or a Camry, and he might have gotten away with it: the front-engine car would have decelerated while pushing—understeering—somewhat into the opposing lanes, but it might have plowed its way around and out of danger. The Porsche swapped ends.

Does this mean Porsches are intrinsically dangerous? No. It means that if you're foolish enough to try it without training, a 911 can corner— or fail to corner—at twice the speed of a Camaro or Camry. *That* can be dangerous.

The 911 has always been a work in progress. Somebody once wrote, "The Porsche 911 is a terrible design brilliantly executed." If any ordinary car had displayed its foibles and faults, the manufacturer would have gone the way of Studebaker, Packard, and American Motors. But Porsche enthusiasts have always happily accepted compromises in aid of lightness, sheer performance, and sharp handling, and most of the 911's mistakes were made during the pursuit of that purity.

God knows the entire car is a compromise, a flawed design in search for half a century of a solution to its tail-happiness. The original Porsche production sports car, the Type 356, was built largely of modified Volkswagen components, particularly the engine. No surprise, since Ferdinand Porsche had designed the VW Beetle. (As well as several *Wehrmacht* tanks, let's not forget.) His layout of that precedential econocar, with the engine actually *behind* the rear axles, its weight partially counterbalanced by a transmission just in front of the axles, was a splendid piece of packaging and presented few problems in a twenty-four-horsepower barely basic car with a top speed of sixty or so.

But. Create a sports car with the same layout, with a four-cylinder VW engine but modified in the 356 to 60, 90, or 120 horsepower, and then on in the 911 to an entirely different engine design—the original 911's flat six—to 150, 180, and more. Way more. The most powerful air-cooled production Porsche 911, the 1999 Turbo S, put down 425 hp, which is your classic order of magnitude—and then some—more powerful than Ferdinand Porsche's original production VW Bug. The Turbo S did, however, have a vastly more sophisticated front and rear independent suspension than the original 911.

In 1973, racer/entrepreneur Roger Penske got the bright idea of initiating a road-racing series called the International Race of Champions—IROC for short—in which absolutely identical race cars would be allocated at random to a dozen or so of the world's top drivers, several from each of the world's totally disparate racing championships. The point was to answer once and for all which series produced the fastest, best drivers—NASCAR, Indy cars, Can-Am road racing, sports cars, or Formula 1.

The machine Penske chose as The Universal Race Car with which to settle the question was the Porsche 911, albeit in a highly modified, 316-horsepower, full-race version called the Carrera RS. This suggested to the editors of *Car and Driver* a snarky, typically *C/D* idea: "Let's get Bobby Allison to track-test the new 1974 Porsche 911 and tell us honestly what he thinks of it."

Allison was one of the NASCAR superstars of the day and was also an IROC competitor. Until he bought a 911 solely to acclimatize himself to it for the IROC series, Alabaman Allison probably had never driven a car with fewer than eight cylinders in a vee. He would have automatically opened a Porsche's trunk to check the oil and popped its engine hatch to bring home his six-packs, so Allison was the perfect spokesman to needle several generations of sporty-car loyalists who mindlessly worshipped at the Porsche altar.

This is not hyperbole. "It is *your* people," Porsche public-relations executive Michael Schimpke said to me once, "who want to come visit Professor Porsche's grave. Even we feel this is strange."

"Compared to American cars that have a good, positive, front-end feel and a back end that just trails along meekly," said Allison in *Car and Driver*, "Porsches are . . . much more aggressive. They are very quick-reacting, almost squirrelly, in what would be a normal maneuver in any other car." It's hard to imagine what a suburban rodent has to do with automotive handling, but "squirrelly" is one of the worst epithets a test driver can apply to an automobile.

"I've driven my [Porsche] pretty fast on Interstate highways," Allison admitted, "and when you get it up to speed, it's pretty comfortable. But you better not move the steering wheel very much. If you want to change lanes at 70, you learn quickly to do it very carefully." Time flies. In 1974, a top pro race car driver considered 70 mph to be "pretty fast" on a public highway. Today, women applying makeup and men doing deals on cell phones routinely commute at 80 in porky, towering SUVs.

"Unlike an American car, the Porsche's back end doesn't trail meekly behind the front," *Car and Driver* elaborated upon Allison's remarks. "And it's this feeling that convinces so many street drivers that they are in the world's best-handling car. At low speeds, city traffic and brisk marches through winding lanes, a 911 is supremely agile. The steering is quick and the car instantly changes direction with only the lightest touch. It feels for all the world like a civilized racer and gives great pleasure. But the Porsche's personality changes drastically as you approach its limit. The tail swings heavily, and the car responds to an unpracticed and unsubtle touch with a vengeance. Moderate street drivers never learn of this; the adventuresome ultimately will find out."

So why, if the thing was such a squirrel, was the 911 the all-conquering production sports-racers throughout the '70s, '80s and at least part of the '90s, before mega-motor Corvettes, Vipers, and even BMWs began to blow them away? "It didn't matter how badly they handled," said my friend Nick Longhi, who makes a living as a hired-gun pro racer —Ferrari this week, Mustang the next, then some wealthy team owner's Porsche—"you just sort of drove around each corner and then blew past everybody on the straight, the Turbos had so much horse-power. And reliability." (Nick, in fact, would be my 911-driving daughter Brook's racing instructor.)

But the 911 was improved, and improved again, and again. Every small model change made it a better car. Porsche put ever-wider tires on the back wheels to keep the rear end in place. They changed the rear-suspension design subtly, to a configuration informally called "the Weissach axle," after the company's engineering center west of Stuttgart, that made the rear wheels toe in slightly whenever the car approached oversteer, thus mitigating its tendency to spin.

Most visibly, Porsche added aerodynamic aids to cure the 911 front end's tendency to float at high speeds and to plant the rear end yet more firmly. This played a big part in making spoilers a *de rigueur* design element on the trunk lids of just about every *poseur* car in the world. When the Porsche Turbo was introduced in 1975, it had what was quickly dubbed a whale tail—an excrescence of a spoiler atop its engine hatch as big and flat as a tea table and looking like freed Willy fleeing for the open sea. It had been preceded by a sassy and more proportionate spoiler on the racing RSR called the ducktail, but only motorheads noticed the ducktail. The whale tail was so over-the-top that everybody had to have one.

My modest 911SC had no whale tail, though that would eventually change. It arrived with just a plain, graceful engine hatch with the classic 911 cooling-air grille and a black badge that growled "911SC."

"Hey," I said to Susan, "let's lose that ugly badge, fill in the fastening holes before we repaint the car, make it even cleaner looking." Nothing doing, she said. My wife's initials are SC.

In fact I was only making like a Good German. The single most common car modification performed by German new-car buyers today involves asking the dealer to strip off the car's model designation numbers or letters from the trunk lid or, in the case of a Porsche 911, the engine-compartment lid. Americans follow the opposite tack, of course, and favor rear ends displaying entire chrome catalogues of their cars' attributes—"4.0-liter V6 twin cam turbocharged/intercooled 24-valve fuel-injected Bose radio full leather XKLX5000 Sport Baronet" and the like.

The Germans, however, had a reason beyond good taste. When the Greens—the forceful environmentalists who have since become a powerful political force in Germany—began badgering rich drivers with fuel-thirsty V12 engines about being politically incorrect, those Mercedes S600 and BMW 750iL owners removed their badges of shame, leaving traffic to wonder whether perhaps the naked-trunked car in front of them was actually a modest Mercedes S320 or six-cylinder BMW 735.

And now the inevitable next step has taken place. Six-cylinder owners remove *their* badges so the neighbors can wonder whether the Schultzes are in fact doing well enough to have bought a twelve. Oh well, if you can't use your car to define your dreams, desires, and imagined accomplishments, what good is it? If all you want is transportation, buy an Opel.

My 911 didn't have a whale tail, but it did have a front spoiler, an inconspicuous rubber-lip air dam below the front bumper that in fact is aerodynamically quite important. Look at the side view of a 911. Look at the side view of an airfoil. They're both flat on the bottom and curved on top, which is how Bernoulli decided that we get lift. Intended in the case of an airplane, unintended in the case of a Porsche.

The SC's air dam keeps air from flowing under the car and turning it into a wing. Unfortunately, lots of 911 owners who know more about style than substance are quick to add high-visibility aftermarket whale tails to their cars without first paying for the front air dam, which is nowhere near big or visible enough to be a chick magnet. Short of putting bigger tires in the front than the back, this is about as squirrelly a configuration as you can create for a 911. The front end wants to lift while the rear end wants to push down. Get the picture?

Chapter Four

DUE DILIGENCE

'd owned two well-used 1950s Porsches. Both were Speedsters, the economy Porsches of the era ($2,999 took one out the dealer's door, if you didn't order any options). But never did I feel I'd someday be lucky enough to own one of the new era of luxury 911 sportsters.

With an arbitrary budget of $10,000 to $15,000 for the initial buy, I nonetheless had the standard Porsche-buyer advice from experts ringing in my ears. "Buy the newest 911 you can afford." So I sought an SC, which was where my price range led me in the Porsche spectrum. An SC coupe, since to my eyes true Porsches have always been closed cars. Since 911 Cabriolets are nice but expensive. Since Targas are basket-handled abominations that go best with gold chains and pinkie rings. John Travolta, playing a cheesy lawyer, drove a Targa in the film *A Civil Action.* Case rests.

I did the research that every serious used-Porsche buyer should do, which consisted in part of reading a splendid little shirt-pocket book called *Buying a Used Porsche 911,* by a long-time Porsche mechanic, Peter Zimmerman. Year by year, Zimmerman exposes each model's faults—overstressed engines, rusty rocker panels, exploding clutches, demonic camchain tensioners, furnace-hot thermal reactors, and a variety of lesser faults.

No 911 model is immune to quirks and failings, but they generally got better (with a few exceptions) as the factory learned from its mistakes.

So unless you're looking for pure collectibility, indeed buy the newest 911 you can afford. Certainly some of the earliest 911s are immensely desirable, with their short wheelbases, lightweight, sportingly spartan accommodations, good balance, and small and efficient engines. But they are rust-prone, delicate, and getting on toward being almost forty years old.

From 1969 through 1973, Porsche even built 911s with two small batteries, one on either side of the nose compartment for ideal balance. Before that, they'd mounted two twenty-pound lumps of lead inside each end of the front bumper in an attempt to counterbalance some of the car's tail-happiness. And you thought German engineering meant high technology.

Some of the mid-'70s models are best avoided because of hot-running engines that had grown awkwardly from 2.0 to 2.7 liters and were warping crankcases, pulling head studs, trashing camchains, and generally acting like sullen teenagers who don't know their own strength. But the major determinant in choosing a proper Porsche is that by 1978, the factory had begun making 911s entirely out of galvanized steel, which, with cautious use during salty winters, ensured that the cars would remain reasonably unrusty for decades. Before that time, Porsches were almost as good as English cars at collecting road salt and trapping it in the water-soaked nooks and crannies of their mild-steel bodies. This ensured that the inevitable chemistry experiment called oxidation would soon take place.

If you're serious about buying a used Porsche, the most important thing to do is what the lawyers who drive Targas call due diligence. Read everything you can find about the various models, so you know enough to ask the seller: "Have you installed a pop-off valve in the airbox? Did you do the Carrera camchain-tensioner update? Does this car have the Dilavar head studs? What are your most recent leakdown-test numbers?" Learn to translate a VIN, the long sequence of letters and numbers that is each individual car's genome. It will tell you where and when the car was built, what its model year is, what its place in that year's sequence of 911s was—early, midyear, or late—and, most important, which world market the car was built for. Some 911s were built to be legal U.S. cars, under DOT and EPA regulations. Some were built for Japan or Canada or "RoW"—Rest of World.

If the VIN tells you that the car you're considering is a RoW car, that means it was brought here as a gray-market car, probably during the 1970s and 1980s, when certain desirable Porsches weren't imported into the U.S., for a variety of reasons, and were brought in by private importers who did quick-and-dirty modifications to allow them to pass U.S. emissions and safety checks.

I remember visiting a gray-market importer once, doing research for a magazine article. The "company" had a grand-sounding name—something like "Trans-Global High Performance Automotive Specialties"— with a fancy Manhattan skyscraper address. When I got there, I found a closet-size office barely big enough to hold the two telephone-wielding Russians who ran the place, both of them smoking evil cigarettes that they held backward between thumb and forefinger. I felt like I was in a bad movie.

Beware: gray-market cars are spoiled goods, always worth from 10 to 30 percent less than their legal equivalents. Unless it's Bill Gates's 959— the ultimate gray-market Porsche—and you can prove it.

The Gates 959 is a particularly infamous Porsche. It is one of a group of 337 Porsche 959s built in the mid-1980s, essentially road-going realizations of everything that Porsche had learned through racing, applied to the 911. All-wheel drive, twin turbochargers, superlight, enormously powerful, to-die-for exotic, and filled with what for the time was cutting-edge suspension-controlling electronics, the 959 was one of the original true supercars.

"Supercar" is today a label applied as indiscriminately as is "supermodel," but the 959 was a kick-ass car that, with a top speed of 197 mph, could sweep the floor with any of the era's Ferraris. It was the fastest and most sophisticated "production" road car of its time and was basically built as a rolling advertisement for Porsche's for-hire engineering capabilities. (It's not widely known that Porsche's engineering center at Weissach will work for food. Porsche engineers have anonymously designed everything from the original five-cylinder Mercedes diesel of the '70s to the 60-degree-vee, four-valve Harley-Davidson V-Rod motorcycle engine.) The 959 was also the precursor of today's all-wheel drive, water-cooled, 424-hp 996 Turbos.

Gates and his Microsoft startup collaborator Paul Allen, in an exuberant display of hubris, bought and had shipped to Seattle in 1987 two brand-new but U.S.-illegal 959s. They had never been crash- or emissions-tested, but I'm guessing that these two Masters of the Universe figured they didn't need no stinkin' DOT or EPA badges and would soon have their heavy-breathing cars on Highway 101 hustling down to Malibu after a few phone calls to friends in high places.

Guess again. The two 959s got no farther than the U.S. Customs Service Port of Seattle impoundment warehouse, where they remained gathering dust, corrosion, and shrinking seals for thirteen years until the DOT/EPA regulations were changed to allow the importation of "Autos of Interest," with strict conditions for their use. Much like the FAA rules governing such things as ex-Soviet MiG fighters and other air-show exotics, these unusual, desirable, usually unique cars are now allowed into the country with a variety of limitations that preclude pretty much everything but their display at car shows and museums.

Chapter Five

PROJECT CAR

I wasn't looking for anything that exotic. At first, my search for an SC went national, with me answering classified ads from all over the country and e-mailing back and forth with brand-new Porsche Internet acquaintances.

Shopping for a Porsche that might be five hundred or a thousand miles away is actually a perfectly reasonable way to search for a project car, particularly in this era of e-mail and instant digital photos. Certainly a snapshot is a pretty superficial look at a $10,000-plus investment, but the Porsche enthusiast network is well-organized and takes itself seriously enough that Porsche Club of America and Porsche Owners Club members can be called upon, sometimes for a small fee, sometimes just for the fun of it, to do a prepurchase inspection for you. If nothing else, some cooperative local chapter member can be counted on to drive the car to a reputable shop that'll do it.

With a project car, you're basically looking for a straight, rust-free platform with a body that hasn't been pastiched with Bondo, plus enough decoding of the VIN to ensure that the car isn't bogus or a gray-market import.

The VIN will tell you the type of engine it should have, what body it was built with, and a variety of other details. After all, Targas have had their roll bar hoops sawed off to turn them into phony Cabriolets. Cabs are worth more than Targas, but only if they have the body-stiffening structure that is part of the legitimate model. You need to know how to decipher a VIN before you go Porsche-shopping, and there are a variety of Porsche books that crack the code. (VIN stands for Vehicle Identification Number, even though everybody calls it "the vin number," which is as redundant as pizza pie or Mount Fujiyama.) It's bad enough that a Porsche's speedometer is about as easy to open as a can of cat food, thus ensuring billions of rolled-back odometer miles floating around out there in the 911 ether, but at least the VIN can help you discover that the car being offered as an '83 SC was actually built in 1979.

Probably at least as important as ensuring that your new Porsche isn't riddled with rust is making damn sure that it never got hit hard enough to get bent. There are easy ways to make this determination, which Peter Zimmerman details in *Buying a Used Porsche 911*. I was particularly primed for this possibility, for I'd naively fallen for a wonky Porsche once before.

It was back in the mid-'60s, when the *über*Porsche was an exotic four-cam-engine version of the original 356. It was called the Carrera—the first use of a decidedly non-German name that ultimately became joined at the hip to the marque Porsche. I found one for sale—a white 356B Speedster, no less, with a rare 1500cc version of the roller-bearing, quad-cam Hirth engine in the back. It was so cheap that I was sure the poor fool who was selling it didn't know the difference between a VW and a Porsche, much less a multicam Carrera, so I snapped it up before anybody else who knew about Porsches got a chance to come in and outbid me.

I had my then-wife drive our new jewel home. She followed me as I drove our other car, and I still remember glancing into the rearview mirror and realizing to my horror that Micheline seemed to be in a four-wheel drift to the left, the entire car cocked five degrees to the right.

I'd bought a dog-tracker.

Dog-tracker? Have you ever watched a mutt trot down the street? Westminister Show hounds may run straight, but most others perambulate with their hindquarters at a slight angle to their direction of travel, perhaps so their rear paws don't kick the fronts. It's also what happens to a car with a chassis bent as the result of a serious accident, hence the dreaded term dog-tracker.

In the old days, pre-1960s, most cars had "frames," which were basically a pair of heavy steel beams that ran the length of the car, one on each side, connected by small lateral beams like the rungs of a ladder and often with a central X of somewhat larger connector members. All of the car's greasy bits—engine, transmission, steering, suspension, rear axle, and differential—were bolted to the frame, and the entire body-and-fenders unit plopped down atop it. You've seen the process in History Channel documentaries about Ford's invention of the assembly line, the grainy film invariably accompanied by a ragtime piano.

Cars got "bent frames" in an accident, and the permanent damage was difficult to see once the bodywork had been repaired. After all, it needed only to be one frame rail imperceptibly bent and everything attached to the chassis was then out of whack.

Today, virtually all cars have platforms rather than frames—a relatively thin sheet-metal affair to which the basic body panels are all welded, forming a very stiff "unibody." Imagine a huge cookie pan with stiffening corrugations and declivities stamped into it, and you have a 911's platform.

It's hard to deform such a platform without the results being evident somewhere. Take a cookie pan and whack one corner with a big mallet. You might be able to smooth out the damage right where the hammer hit the metal, but if it deformed the pan—the platform—there's going to be a ripple, a wrinkle, a bulge somewhere.

Clean-bellied little Porsches, fortunately, are easy to check for frame damage. Put a 911 up on a garage lift and its past is pretty clear. Unfortunately, I didn't know that back when I was a naïf thinking that in the cheap 356 Carrera Speedster I'd come across in a *Philadelphia Inquirer* classified, I'd found a deal too good to be true. Which in fact is exactly what I had found. I painted the car refrigerator-white, the color most effective at hiding irregular bodywork, and eventually sold it to a kid even dumber than I was.

Chapter Six

NO WARRANTY, NO NOTHING

ltimately, I found my car just sixty miles from home, in Long Island City, a shabby New York neighborhood near LaGuardia Airport, amid sidewalks littered with broken bottles, bodegas on the corners, and stripped cars perched on milk crates at every other curb. The dealer was an Indian, perhaps a Pakistani, and his wares, though advertised in *Hemmings* as "exoticars," were a motley collection of dreadful Jaguar Mark sedans, ugly entry-level Ferraris, Cobra kit cars, shabby Royces and Bentleys, *poseur* Panteras, neglected Porsches— yes, a lot of Targas—and phony fiberglass MGs. They were packed grille to bumper, fender to dusty fender in a dim, foul warehouse. The mechanical expertise of the place seemed limited to jumping dead batteries.

"Hiya. I'm here to look at the red Porsche coupe? The '83 that you're advertising for ten five?" I said to the owner.

"Oh, dear me, sir" he grimaced. "It is a very nice car, but it is $11,500 and not a penny less." I had planned to start at $9,000 and maybe end up at $10,000—an excellent deal for a year and model that sold for twice that in perfect condition.

"Gee, you faxed me that it was $10,500, and I made the trip all the way down here on that basis," I said.

"I would certainly like to see *that* fax," he countered.

See it he did, since I'd brought it with me. "Huh," he grunted.

The car was a sad little rat. The mechanic started it, and it idled smokily at a warm-up setting, the haphazard Porsche threshing-machine clatter a sound that brought back memories. The interior was shabby, the driver's leather seat split, the carpeting bunched and filthy, the glare-shield terminally cracked, the rear-bulkhead paneling waterlogged and crumbling, loose wires showing the harsh removal of an aftermarket amplifier and a boom box speaker rig that had been parked crudely on the jump-seat cushions, the engine compartment slick with spilled oil, the air-conditioner hoses dangling loose, the Guards Red paint cracked and faded where the Neanderthal PO (previous owner, in Porschespeak) had rigged a nose-protecting bra and then never removed it. The driver's door sagged half an inch when opened, so he was probably fat as well, accustomed to using the door as a crutch.

Perfect.

I took the headlights out of their fender bowls to look for hidden rust. Ran a magnet all over the body to test for Bondo, the sandable plastic paste that body shops trowel over crash damage they can't be bothered to smooth. (The magnet would stick to steel but not Bondo, of course.) Parked the car so that the sunlight hit it at the right angle to give away bodywork ripples when I sighted along the fenders and doors. Checked the VIN to find that the car had been built during the summer of 1983 in Stuttgart for the U.S. market—a very late SC, one of the last of the breed. Checked the engine number to confirm that it was the correct engine for the year. Looked for the dreaded spilled-acid corrosion under the battery tray. Jacked the car up and poked an awl at the bellypan in some famously vulnerable areas to check for rust-thinned metal . . .

"I've never seen anybody do all that," the dealer said—either admiringly or calculatedly, hoping to make me think I actually knew what I was doing.

I drove the thing around for barely five minutes simply to make sure it actually ran and tracked straight. No need to check compression, valve leakage, gearbox crunching, shock stiffness, or tire condition. The tires were Sumitomos, a Japanese off-brand famed only for their cheapness and excellent adaptability to use as boat–dock bumpers. I had no interest in any of the obvious things that used-car buyers concern themselves with, for all of those components would be renewed, rebuilt, replaced before the car ever ran again.

Ship it, I told the shabby dealer. Put the thing on a flatbed and send it to me. Oh, and how about a discount for not asking for a warranty? "Warranty?" he laughed. "*Warranty?* No such thing, my man. You can bring your mechanics, you can examine the car all you wish, you can drive and test and check, but you buy and it is yours. Don't come back. No warranty. No nothing."

Well, what the hell. It's a project car, not a grocery-getter.

Chapter Seven

WHAT LARRY RIVERS
NEVER KNEW

A week later, my Porsche showed up at our Hudson Valley home strapped to a flatbed. Within minutes, the red coupe was on the ground, the freight bill paid, and the truck gone. Key, crank, start, a short trip up the long driveway, and my project car was home, only briefly to run again until it was a brand-new, totally restored 1983 911SC.

What in God's name had I signed up for? In front of me sat a small coupe poised like a hunkered-down toad on its wide, high-speed, Z-rated tires. It was a machine that many people consider to be so incomprehensibly complex that it should only be worked on by people named Dieter and Rolf, imperious Teutons in white shopcoats. Tattered as it was, this was a *Porsche,* made of aluminum and magnesium, leather and fine steel, hand-assembled in Stuttgart in annual numbers that would have sufficed for a day's production of Ford Tauruses.

What right did I have to tamper with such a jewel?

I grew up as a teenager in the late 1940s and that Silent Decade, the 1950s—years that I remember as stretching from Levittown to the Kingston Trio. My mother was a women's-magazine writer, a kind of early-day Martha Stewart, and one how-to article she wrote when I was a boy involved a family that built just the basement of their house, put a flat roof atop it, and lived in that below-ground cellar, perhaps twelve inches of it showing above the sod, while they saved the money to build the rest of the house. That was considered to be adventuresome in those days.

But cars *were* exciting, and I grew up being fascinated by them. Buicks with portholes in the hood—and every kid knew exactly how many holes a Limited had and how many marked the Special. (Four and three, or was it the reverse? I no longer remember.) The first "modern" Ford, the 1949 three-box car, as the design concept is now known—engine box, passenger box, and trunk box, arrayed one after the other so the car's front and rear were relatively symmetrical, a remarkable concept in those days. The which-way-is-it-going '47 Studebaker, styled by Raymond Loewy and so impossibly futuristic that it was hard to tell front from rear. (You called a Studebaker a Stoopandtakeit to show your car-guy coolness.) The Henry J, a forgotten little cutie that was a compact twenty years before the category was invented. Bulbous Kaiser-Frasers, tiny Crosley Hotshots, impossibly ugly dung-beetle Nashes that were the inevitable subject of dirty jokes because their front seats folded flat to make a double bed.

My family had, of all things, a 1930s Packard V12 roadster that my father had converted into a kind of truck, with a wooden box extending out of the lidless trunk, so my Martha Stewart-y mother could carry refinished furniture from her workshop to the pseudoantiques store that she ran. Classic-car collectors have a special circle of Hades for people who turn V12 Packards into pickups, but back then, it was just a used car.

My brother Kirk, then five, once got angry at Mom and threatened to "get out of the car" if she didn't do whatever it was he wanted. "Oh, right, that'll be the day," she said, since they were already rumbling along Baldwin Road at 20 mph.

Old Packards had doors hinged at the back rather than the front, called suicide doors—presumably because that's what might happen to you if you tried what Kirk did. He called her bluff by pushing down the door handle, and the instant the door cracked open the wind caught it, flung it wide, and jerked my brother out of the car.

It was his *second* fractured skull, poor kid. He'd earned the first one when the head came off an ax my father was using to chop down a tree and caught Kirk spang on the forehead. He survived them both to become a hard-headed New Hampshire architect and classic-motorcycle restorer.

My first car, more than fifty years ago, was a 1932 Ford sedan. It didn't run, but I bought it for $25, and the delighted seller towed it to the big barn behind my parents' house and quickly disappeared. I was fourteen. I disassembled as much as I could of the car with my father's tools, cleaned and polished the parts, and reassembled everything. The car still didn't run.

My father said that enough was enough, the car would have to go to the junkyard, where at least I'd get $5 for it. The junkyard of choice was about five miles away. Dad pushed me out to the end of our driveway with his little war-surplus Jeep and nudged me out onto Baptist Church Road, since it was downhill for a little ways.

I remember him telling the story years later. "I followed Stevie down the hill, figuring I'd meet him at the bottom and push that damn Ford to the junkyard, but I went around the first corner, no Stevie. Kept going. Few more corners, kept going, no sight of him. I finally caught up with him at the junkyard."

I'd given the Ford its head, never touched the brakes. The first hill was enough to propel me to a crazed sixty or so—a rarely seen pace in 1950—and I somehow got the old Ford around the country-road corners and let momentum build so that, like a roller coaster, there was always enough to get me to the next downhill. I was collecting my $5 by the time Dad drove up.

Not long after that, my father headed down the same hill in our peasoup-green Chevrolet sedan, on his way to a Wednesday-evening church meeting. Later, much later, he reappeared in the driveway, the car chugging and bucking all the way back up the hill.

My heart sank, for I had that day removed the Chevy's little single-barrel carburetor and "cleaned" it. A carburetor needs a bath about as much as a cat does, but I'd detailed the damn thing till it shone. I never knew how to leave well enough alone—still don't—and am fortunate I didn't try to disassemble the thing as well. Other kids grew up playing with matches, collecting baseball cards, or playing cowboys and Indians. I, remember, took things apart.

Unfortunately, when I replaced the carb on the car, I hooked the throttle rod to the choke and the choke control to the throttle. Dad was able to make the car move, very slowly, by pumping the gas pedal, which coarsely richened the fuel mixture enough to briefly get it going, but he never figured out that he'd have been able to drive it like a dream simply by pulling out the choke. It would have worked fine. He'd even have made it to church.

My next car, three years later, when I actually had a driver's license, was also a Ford, but a very special one, and it eventually was to establish my lack of talent as an engine-builder.

It was a 1936 Ford Phaeton, today among classic Fords possibly the single most-prized model and year. Phaetons are four-door convertibles—they look like claw-foot bathtubs on wheels—with plastic-windowed side curtains rather than roll-up windows. Very sporty. Very leaky. Very breezy.

Back in 1953, when "car collector" meant a family that had two cars, a '36 Ford Phaeton was simply a Ford, and a rather silly one at that. In fact, my father's best friend—William Maxwell, the fiction editor of *The New Yorker*—had stored the car in our barn during winters, and he *gave* me the Phaeton when he finally bought a new car, probably because he was amused by my aberrant interest in such machinery.

Bill Maxwell was one of the most influential magazine editors of the postwar era, though his influence was usually felt by the likes of J. D. Salinger, John Updike, and Eudora Welty rather than by a high-school kid with a car jones. (And years later by my youngest brother, Alec Wilkinson, a *New Yorker* contributor whom Bill Maxwell shaped into a writer of enormous sensitivity and introspection.) Nonetheless, Bill and his gift would ultimately play a part in my being made the editor of an automobile magazine and then, after I was fired for general crankiness, insubordination, and out-of-fashion pants, my becoming a freelance writer often covering affairs automotive.

Bill was the gentlest man I've ever known, almost feminine in his graces and style. He tended rosebushes at his tiny country house down the road from ours and used the Phaeton's radio solely to listen to the Saturday-afternoon Metropolitan Opera broadcast. Inevitably there was gossip among neighbors who assumed he was gay—a word that hadn't yet been turned to that purpose—but Bill eventually fooled them by marrying one of the most beautiful women I've ever known.

The dear man probably was shocked by what I did to his car. First I removed the muffler so that it roared like a broken John Deere, though I fancied that it sounded just like a race car, and then I had it painted British Racing Green with glaringly white wire wheels. It had been a delicate, muted ochre yellow, like one of Bill's roses.

I had a summer job on Cape Cod, working at the Mobilgas station in Wellfleet, and took the Ford with me. The car soon became all too well known, and the Wellfleet Police made me reinstall the muffler.

At the gas station, I learned to do grease jobs, clean spark plugs, mount tires, work the lift, and change customers' engine oil. And I learned what "range oil" was.

On one of my first days at work, a customer showed up with a five-gallon can and asked me to fill it with "drainage oil." At least that's what it sounded like to me, so I went out back to the tank where we collected the dirty oil we'd drained from crankcases and filled his can.

"How much?" he asked.

"Oh, nothin'," I said. "You can have it."

Since he thought he was pulling a fast one on the new kid, it served him right that he went home and poured it into the tank of his kitchen stove, which burned kerosene—"range oil." What a mess.

I took the Phaeton with me to Harvard and spent more time working on it than I did in class. Years after I graduated, barely, my then-father-in-law met a guy who turned out to be a classmate, and Max said to him, "Did you know Steve Wilkinson?" The young man thought about it, ran through his mental Rolodex, and said, "Yes! He was that guy who was always under a green car on Mt. Auburn Street."

Another classmate sold me a hot-rodded Mercury engine for some ludicrous amount—I seem to recall $50—but the little flathead V8 was in pieces, literally a basket case. I assembled it using what few tools I had, and one wintry evening I finally fired it up. (Yes, on Mt. Auburn Street.) It started, and gleefully I drove the thing about three miles. Which is as far as it got before blowing all of its oil out the breather pipe. I had neglected to replace a crucial part, the oil-pressure relief spring, when I built the engine.

My next foray into engine-building went little better, even though this time I chose to minister to just the top end of a simple two-cylinder BSA motorcycle engine. I'd crashed the bike and broken a number of the cylinder barrel's cooling fins, so I needed to replace the barrel before selling the damn thing. (Farewell to motorcycles, at least until a Ducati 350 Desmo road racer tempted me ten years later, but that's another story.)

With everything gleaming and the bike freshly rebarrelled—and what the hell, let's throw in a couple of sets of new piston rings while we're at it—the Beezer sold quickly, to none other than abstract expressionist painter Larry Rivers, then the toast of the pre-yuppie Hamptons.

Rivers owned an Aston Martin DB4 that somebody had given him as payment for a painting. The car was a mess, its svelte aluminum body dinged and dented, the leathery interior looking as though a hard-drinking, beach-bumming, bisexual Greenwich Village beatnik had lived in it, which was pretty much the case.

Rivers had little idea what the car was worth and probably wasn't even aware that *Goldfinger* had just been released, making the obscure Aston Martin marque as much a household name as James Bond's. So I traded him my BSA and not very much money for the Aston. Suddenly, I owned my first exoticar.

My quick trip from the Upper West Side to Rivers's Village studio was my last ride on the BSA, and a dreadful one it was: the engine began to seize, and I barely made it to Rivers's place. Hoping that it was a temporary aberration and that the engine would free up when Larry rode the bike, I took the title to the DB4 and ran. (I'd neglected to check the end-gap of the new piston rings, I later figured—I didn't even know there *was* such a thing as a proper end gap—and they were swelling against the cylinder walls as they heated, with too little space to allow for the expansion.)

The phone rang the next morning. It was, of course, Larry Rivers. "I have terrible news," he said. Tell me about it, I thought to myself: you can't even get it to turn over to start . . . "The bike was stolen last night. I never got a chance to ride it."

I've been wondering ever since how far the unsuspecting thief got before the thing froze solid.

Chapter Eight

WHEN FERDINAND CAME TO CORNWALL

I was somewhat richer, definitely older, and perhaps even smarter when, nearly forty years later, I began work on the Porsche. The restoration process started almost immediately, right there in the driveway, on an unseasonably warm March morning. I stripped the interior—waterlogged carpeting, old road maps, $1.50 in change, decade-old toll receipts, cracked leather paneling, junk scattered in the trunk . . . what's this box? Security system.

God, do I hate "security systems," that most idiotic and ineffectual of automotive options. I once sat in an outdoor café in New Orleans while a pack of Harleys accelerated up the block with enough vigor to set off the alarms of every car they passed. In New York City, security systems are simply devices that make a great deal of noise while a car is being broken into, in effect announcing, "I'm stealing this car. You got a problem with that?"

No sir, I don't. Not at all. You go right ahead and steal that prick-on-the-inside Porsche and don't for an instant consider the possibility of my voluntarily interfering in a city where schoolchildren carry Glocks. Have a nice day, and thank you for getting that noisy car out of here.

In any case, the idiotic security system was gone in sixty seconds, powerless against my wire-snipping pliers. It was quickly trash-canned along with the water-soaked floor carpets.

Uh-oh.

They call these things "immobilizers," don't they? Because they somehow immobilize the car? Right. Now the starter would crank, but the engine wouldn't fire. The Porsche was dead, immovable, a big red lump sitting in the driveway. I had performed what was basically a Porsche heart transplant without having an organ donor lined up.

Some years earlier, I'd built an airplane with a necessarily complex system of radios and electric motors. It had forced me to learn to read normal electrical schematics. Unfortunately, Porsche's enormously expensive factory manuals ($600 for the set covering my car) use a diagrammatic system I'd never seen before. It is sensible, linear, Germanic . . . and utterly incomprehensible until you figure it out. Rather than being trackable on one page from the beginning of each wire to its terminus, wires simply stop in space, terminating in little symbols, "III 25" and "V 7" and the like. Finally it came to me: go to page III and look along the 1-to-30 ruler across the bottom of the page. Find 25 and there will be a symbol, say, "II 15," meaning the wire you're picking up at this point disappeared into the ether on page II at marker 15. Eureka.

Now I could try and figure out what on earth my late lamented security system had affected to keep the car from running. Brown wire, red wire, goes-nowhere wire . . . aha. Fuel pump. Makes sense.

The car ran after I temporarily bridged a few wiring gaps, but not very well. Well enough, while I pumped the throttle, that I was able to barely scoot it from the driveway across the lawn, hard right through a gap in the shrubs and past our little swimming pool without putting a wheel into the muddy brook that crosses the backyard, and pop across the little bridge to the barn that a long-ago farmer built so he could garage the family Model A.

The Ford's oil stains were still faintly visible in the thick, sagging, hoof-chipped planking of the old cow barn. Years ago, a former tenant of our house had appeared one rainy day on our lawn, shyly snapping photos of his old home, and he'd pointed the old puddles out to me, as well as the initials he'd carved into a doorpost in the '40s. He'd been born on a table in the kitchen in 1936, he told me.

Little did he—or I—then know that someday a Porsche would commingle some of its own oil with the Ford's.

His father's Model A was the offspring of the original people's car, the Ford Model T, a car that sold at one time for $550, a price that Henry Ford intended would be affordable for every salaried workman in the country. Ferdinand Porsche, the engineer who designed the original Porsche 356—his son Ferry was running the company by the time the 911 was designed—took this Model T lesson to heart when Hitler asked him (did Hitler ever "ask"?) to come up with a German people's car. A "Volkswagen."

Ferdinand Porsche came to the United States in October of 1936— I was exactly six months old—to see what Mr. Ford and his assembly lines were up to. Porsche, accompanied by an interpreter, had a generally lousy time. The train from New York City to Detroit was slow and coarse compared to German trains, Detroit was even uglier than it is today, and in both Manhattan and Detroit, their hotel rooms weren't ready when they arrived. "Worse yet," reported writer Jerry McDermott in an article in the Porsche-enthusiast magazine *Excellence,* "they only found this out [in Detroit] after a porter took them to a room in which guests were still sleeping."

The proud German engineer got an even bigger shock when he visited General Motors. At one point, his guide lost his way in the headquarters building, McDermott wrote, and needed to ask a receptionist for directions. The young woman ignored the men because she was chatting with a friend, and to Porsche's dismay, his guide refused to interrupt her—it would be impolite, the GM man said to a furious Porsche, who apparently subscribed to the German *Kinder, Kuchen, Kirche* theory of women's place in the world.

Ferdinand Porsche bought himself a new Packard while he was in Detroit, for a nice round $1,000; it was a six rather than one of the fancy V12s. He and his interpreter decided to drive it back to New York. They visited Niagara Falls and headed east to Albany, then south along the Hudson to cross into Manhattan on the spectacular new George Washington Bridge.

There is only one road Ferdinand Porsche could have taken south from Albany: Route 9W, since the New York State Thruway wouldn't be built until well after World War II. To this day, I wonder whether, as his Packard labored up Storm King Mountain on 9W, he might have glanced to the south and seen a small red barn about 500 feet from the road. That barn would someday be mine.

Chapter Nine

TRACK TIME

Route 9W is my mother road, a convenient highway for someone like me, who tests and writes about cars. Lightly trafficked except at rush hour, when commuters from the U.S. Military Academy, at West Point, hurry home, it sweeps for a dozen miles toward and past our home through a series of both sweeping and tight bends and several long straightaways.

One straight is particularly fortuitous. The highway is divided by a concrete barrier at that point, two lanes on each side, with no way for a police car to make a U-turn and chase a speeder. When the road is empty it's where I check cars for high-speed handling, for at the end of a sprint to triple-digit speed, I can turn off onto the tiny, inconspicuous, forest-veiled lane that leads to our house while—and this has happened several times—the trooper wails past wondering where the Lexus with California plates has gone.

But street racing, car against car, I'll never do.

Somewhere out there is a kid in a red BMW 325 with a ski rack who thinks he spanked my 911. He came up on my rear bumper one afternoon looking for a fight, blew past at 65 and wailed away at what looked like about 90. This happened out on the local four-lane—curvy Route 9W. Bimmer boy is probably wondering why a poseur has a rollbar and speed-

equipment stickers on his rear quarter window yet drives like he votes in St. Petersburg. As I watched him disappear into the distance, I thought to myself, "Have a nice day, 2Fast 2Stupid, I'm going to the track tomorrow."

When I first wrote those words, as part of a monthly column I do for *Popular Science* magazine, the issue hadn't been on the newsstands for more than a few days before I got one e-mail from an annoyed St. Petersburg booster, which was to be expected, and another from the guy in the red BMW, which wasn't.

Popular Science used to print my actual address at the end of each of my "Man and Machine" columns, until I did one on handguns and got tired of an inbox flooded with messages from gun nuts calling me everything from a Commie liberal to a faggot. So now they publish an address that takes the e-mails directly to the magazine, where the crazed and slanderous messages are filtered out and the relatively reasonable ones forwarded to me. The BMW guy was polite enough to pass muster.

He'd recognized himself, at least in part because he remembered my by-then locally infamous yellow Porsche, and because there's only one 9W. He reminded me that in fact I'd stood on the gas as he pulled out to pass me, and that we were both having a good time till I backed off. And that he wasn't "a kid," goddammit, he was thirty.

That's a kid to this silverback, but I replied that perhaps my poetic license should be revoked. Which turned out to be appropriate: Dave Wingfield is a cop in a nearby town and has a sense of humor. We've since become friends, but next time I tell a national audience about getting passed by a red BMW, I'll turn it into a green Saab.

In any case, I *was* going to the track the next day and saw no need to risk a ticket on a public road. No, I'll never be a racer. I'm way too inept to ever bang fenders, but every couple of months, for about $100 a day, I rent Lime Rock, Watkins Glen, or Pocono and go play. Or, if it's her turn, daughter Brook drives the little yellow coupe.

How is that possible?

Okay, I exaggerate. The truth is that I and about 150 other drivers rent each track, under the auspices of the Porsche Club of America.

The C-note—the cost varies a bit depending on the track and the sponsoring PCA region—is the fee to participate in a "Driver Education" day, which basically involves driving around the track as fast as you're able to, with a club instructor, who is usually a serious amateur racer, in the right seat.

One of the best-kept secrets of enthusiast driving is that a number of car clubs besides the Porsche Club do much the same thing, and some of them welcome a variety of other models as well. Just about every enthusiast car brand (or "marque," as the pretentious style it) has a well-organized national club that puts together everything from local barbecues to national races and car beauty shows for members. The driver-education (DE) events are low-key and noncompetitive, and nobody worries about whether you're a moving speed bump or an incipient Michael Schumacher.

Cars are allowed to pass only on selected straights and after the slower driver has signaled when and where to pass. You're driving as fast as you're able, yet it's safer than the drive *to* the track. Everybody is going in the same direction, nobody's talking on a cell phone or applying makeup, road rage has been left far behind, and there are ample grassy areas for spinouts if you do lose control.

A willingness to learn, to have a good time, and a helmet are the only requirements. If you're confident and reasonably skilled, you may end up driving 120 or more mph for the first time in your life. One middle-aged Porsche owner came back into the parking area after his first-ever laps at a racetrack in Lime Rock, Connecticut, rhapsodizing, "That is *fantastic!* I've never even gone over 70 before!"

Here's how it happens.

Oh-seven hundred on a ceiling-zero foggy June morning in Watkins Glen, New York: I find my way from the woodsy Seneca Lodge to the track and, as always, am humbled by the variety of Porsches already present. My '83 is a creaky antique among Twin Turbos, full-race Cup cars, GT2s, and specials that have arrived in enclosed trailers. But never mind, there are also Boxsters with childish-scrawl friction-tape numbers on their doors, older guys in brand-new water-pumper 996s who can barely parallel-park, and a harried woman in a Targa who can't find the tech-inspection line.

Porsche Club instructor Jim Lewis jumps into my car and says, "We're gonna have *fun* today!" His enthusiasm is strangely calming, and as our line of M&M-colored cars snakes out onto the track, Jim talks me through "the line." Cars are divided into four or five groups depending on driver experience. The higher categories can circulate without instructors if they choose. I, of course, am in the St. Petersburg Class. Which has nothing to do with Russian nobility and everything to do with the elderly couple that always comes to my mind when the subject of Florida drivers arises.

This is not an urban legend. It actually happened. Two aged Floridians, creeping through St. Pete toward I-275, suddenly saw what they were seeking—the broad concrete of the interstate. A hard left and they were on their way, through a conveniently open gate and directly onto the main runway of St. Petersburg International Airport. While landing aircraft were hastily ordered by the tower to go around, the geezers motored happily toward New Jersey or whatever their destination was, but all too soon plunged directly into Tampa Bay somewhat past the point where they should properly have lifted off and begun their climb to cruise altitude. Fortunately, the airport fire department was having a drill nearby and pulled them out.

"There are four keys to driving fast," Lewis says. "Line, smoothness, vision, and focus."

Line is obvious: the one best way through a corner, cutting an arc from turn-in to apex (the point where you clip the inside verge) to track-out so that you don't lose any more speed than necessary and come out of the corner as fast as possible. Fast out is *way* better than fast in. "Apex late is great," racers say, because then you're pointed pretty much toward whatever straight follows. Apex early and you'll be scrubbing around the next two-thirds of the turn losing speed.

Smoothness entirely escapes go-for-it street racers and is hard for novice closed-course road racers to achieve as well. Smoothness means maintaining the chassis's balance. Whenever you hit the brakes, stab the throttle, or turn the steering wheel the car pitches, yaws, or rolls around its center of gravity. Brake hard and the car bobs forward, putting lots of weight on the front tires but lightening the rears . . . which might then begin to slide sideways and spin. Whack the gas to the floor coming out of a corner and the reverse happens, lightening the front wheels and making it harder for them to steer. Jerk the steering wheel and the car suddenly throws its weight to one side or the other, which doesn't help directional control either.

So brake firmly but progressively, and in a straight line, not while turning; don't ask the front wheels to do two things at once. Don't jump on the gas; squeeze it like a trigger. And steer smoothly, not making macho corrections and countersteers just to look cool.

Vision is another tough one. Most of us stare at the inside curb of the corner we're going through, concentrating on the apex. Then, when we clip it, we look up and start thinking about the next one. Bad idea. When you're into a corner and have established your arc to the apex, be looking for the track-out point. And as soon as you know where track-out is, look for the next corner. The odd thing is that a car will tend to go where you're looking. There's a strange kinesthetic feedback between eyeballs and hands on the wheel.

Focus? It simply means don't let your mind wander. "I've done it myself," Lewis says. "You start thinking, 'Oh, man, I really nailed that corner, I'm an ace, I'm so cool,' and before you know it, you're into the next turn too fast or off line." Only a racer knows how physically and mentally hard it is to stay focused, and whenever you hear someone say, "NASCAR drivers? How hard can it be to turn left?" you can be pretty sure it's an overweight, out-of-shape, stick-and-ball spectator. They have no clue.

With driver Tom Kristensen at the wheel, I recently strapped myself into the tiny passenger seat of a serious, dedicated, world-class race car—the 600-horsepower, 215-mph Bentley Speed 8 that in 2003 won the 24 Hours of Le Mans. Kristensen is a handsome young Dane (there I go again, he's in his mid-thirties) who was part of that very Le Mans-winning team, and Tom and I were on a racetrack in southern Spain.

The speeds we reached didn't surprise me. I've been in lots of fast cars, ridden in race cars before, and have spent a fair amount of time myself driving at 150 mph and more on Autobahns, invitingly empty highways, and racetracks. But the brutality of this experience reminded me why all race car drivers truly are athletes.

The brakes on a modern race car (in combination with the rubber of its very special tires) are its most powerful system. Literally. Race car engines typically generate 600 to 900 motive horsepower, but their brakes generate the equivalent of *thousands* of absorptive hp. It's one thing to ride at 150 mph. It's another to ride at 150 mph toward a hard right corner only several car lengths ahead and realize that you're somehow going to slow down and round it alive.

I once rode with a very experienced Texas crop duster in a big old Stearman PT-17 biplane while he demonstrated the dusting maneuvers that he flew for a living. We rumbled along the rows of a bean field, the big radial engine chuttering away, so low that I was almost at eye level with the bemused field hands leaning on their hoes. At the end of the field was a two-lane road, bordered on the near side by telephone poles and wires, and on the far side by a row of trees.

"Oh, OK," I remember thinking, "we're so close, obviously we're going to fly under the wires and straight through the trees. What the hell, I trust this guy to get away with that."

We indeed flew under the phone lines, but in the width of a country road, the guy racked the Stearman into a climb that cleared the oncoming trees by inches.

I felt the same confidence every time Tom Kristensen got on the Bentley's brakes. "Oh, OK, we're gonna die, but I trust this guy to get away with that." The G-loads were so intense that my neck ached and my crash helmet constantly wobbled like a bobble-head doll. I had to hang on to a small metal handle not to stay in place—a torture-tight six-point seatbelt/shoulder harness took care of that—but simply to keep my arms from flinging themselves around the cockpit and interfering with Kristensen's work. By the end of the ride, my fingers were close to bleeding.

Only fighter pilots experience anything like the G-loads that a serious racer undergoes when braking—up to 4Gs in a Formula 1 car—and not even a Tomcat Top Gun does it for hours at a time.

Tom Kristensen does it for a living, but why do rank amateurs like me take our Porsches to the track? Never mind the idiotic Vin Diesel street-racing movies, these days you can't turn on a television or open a car-enthusiast magazine without seeing either SUVs achieving new levels of off-road silliness or sports sedans carving corners, tachs at the redline, perfectly manicured hands slamming the shifters, and magically traffic-free roads blurred by speed. Forget about "closed course, professional driver, don't try this at home," we're still an automotive culture encouraged to make use of the capability of cars fast enough to get an ordinary driver into a world of hurt. Yet aside from the tiny minority who attend expensive performance-driving schools, we are for the most part automotive klutzes.

To do something about it, all drivers need do is join a national one-make car club—Porsche, Audi, Mustang, Corvette, Jaguar, Miata, and on and on—which usually costs around $50 a year. Wanna race? They aren't going to let you on the track with your mother's Crown Vic, but if you drive a car with sporting pretensions—even a red BMW 325 four-door with a ski rack—you can probably find a group that'll let you aboard.

Chapter Ten

CREATIVE CURSING

I f you write checks to car-restoration specialists rather than working on the car yourself, you'll never get your fingernails dirty. Never get leaky scabs on your knuckles when a wrench slips and you slice off a dime-sized piece of skin. Never learn why those piston rings need to have very specific end gaps. Never have to stand there looking at the sorry pieces of what was once a car and think, "*Now* what?" That's a pity.

You'll also never learn truly creative cursing. When I was building an airplane in the same red barn a decade ago, some recalcitrant parts and pieces needed to be sworn into place. My wife's parents came to stay with us each August, just when the work was hottest, sweatiest, and sweariest. (They had retired to Florida and considered our New York home an Arctic refuge.) Grace and Irwin would sit in the living room and read or watch tennis tournaments on TV, the patio doors wide open, facing the distant barn.

"It's a shame Stephan is having such an awful time with that airplane," Grace one day said to Susan.

"Why do you say that?" Susan asked. "He *loves* that work."

"But he uses the most awful language all the time," Grace said. "It's really embarrassing to hear, all those F and C words . . ."

I'd thought myself safe, all alone to curse creatively, but the barn apparently had odd acoustic properties, a big wooden Bose that broadcast my epithets clearly across the lawn to my shocked in-laws. It reminded me of the time my father, during a take-your-kid-to-work day when I was twelve, showed me a spot in a broad, busy, vaulted area in Grand Central Station where, if each of us faced a corner a good 50 feet apart, we could clearly hear our whispers travel an arc across the tile-lined ceiling even while hordes of commuters shuffled past. Acoustics 101.

Certainly if somebody is restoring a truly valuable collectible car—which a 1983 Porsche 911SC definitely isn't—they should take advantage of experts to do the things that no do-it-yourselfer's shop is truly equipped to do, such as rechroming, serious bodywork, and replication of missing parts.

But I was intent on doing this car myself, with my own hands and tools.

"*You* can't overhaul a 911 engine," some experts told me. "It takes years of experience to work on these complex, expensive, close-tolerance machines. It's not like some crude American V8. Why do you think they gave me a clipboard and a white shopcoat with my name on the pocket?"

Discouraging. But a few others said, "Go for it. Take your time, read everything you can get your hands on, keep everything scrupulously clean, and whenever you're not sure of something, ask questions."

A modest, unassuming Porsche specialist in Portland, Oregon, named Steve Weiner was among the few. Weiner is one of the country's most respected builders of high-performance street and competition Porsche 911s. He runs a shop in Portland called Rennsport Systems *(www.rennsport-systems.com)* that builds and modifies extremely fast and powerful 911s for customers who can afford the work, a lot of them software and Internet-enrichened techies from the Northwest. Though he in Oregon and I in New York were a continent apart, I was fortunate to find in him a friend.

Weiner could answer any question I had, but when they were too minor to bother him with, I went to the Net. Twenty years ago, my only resources would have been making friends at the local "foreign-car shop" that once worked on a Porsche or two, or a Porsche dealership forty miles away that wouldn't talk to me anyway. Or at best, endless phone calls to Porsche Club of America members in my area who, if I caught them home, might or might not have some advice.

But now I'm plugged into half the Porsche-savvy enthusiasts on the planet. The Internet is filled with Porsche-specific bulletin boards and chat rooms; type "Porsche" into Google and you'll be inundated.

Proceed with caution, however. These posting sites are frequented by a few of the world's most knowledgeable Porsche techies, but also by lots of people who think they know more about Porsches than they in fact do. As is true of virtually all Internet information, what you learn will cost you nothing and may well be worth exactly that. There are drudges out there whose lives revolve around checking into their Porsche bulletin boards five and six times a day so that they can demonstrate their expertise by answering innocent technical queries with responses that could turn your 911 engine into a big aluminum grenade.

Taking a car apart is easy. Far easier than putting it back together again. I delightedly tore into the messy disassembly job, since it was my ez-on/ez-off introduction to the task of automobile restoration I removed everything inside the cabin from the dirty, tattered headliner to the thick, sprayed-on soundproofing on the floor. Ripping stuff out is a gorilla's job. Replacing it requires skills I wasn't yet concerned that I might lack.

Somewhere I'd heard that the floorpan soundproofing, a kind of hardened tar, weighed a total of sixteen pounds. People who turn 911s into dedicated race cars take it out by freezing it with dry ice, after which it supposedly flakes off easily. My car's sound-deadening layer came out with slightly more effort and the persuasive powers of a strong putty knife, but it flaked off cleanly, in taffylike chunks. I didn't bother collecting and weighing the pieces, figuring I'd take the word of others, even if I did learn it on the Internet.

All of the waterlogged carpeting went into the trash, as did two small wooden floorboards at the very front of the cabin. They were ordinary German plywood that had been water soaked along their bottom edges for years and were terminally warped and separated between the plies. What a throwback: the 911 must have been just about the only car on earth in 1983—other than the British Morgan roadster—to still utilize wood in its construction. Nineteen eighty-three? Good lord, those two pieces of plywood remained a part of the design until the water-cooled 996 was introduced as a 1999 model.

Today, various aftermarket suppliers sell carbon-fiber and drilled-aluminum-alloy replacement floorboards, but I didn't know that yet so I reverted to the original. No problem: they'll probably rot out again in a decade, since 911s are famously leaky in the rain, and then I can modernize.

One of the beauties of the 911 is that many of the model's components, such as the windshield and side glass, remained identical for decades. The bad news is that so did some of the car's most archaic features, such as those rot-prone plywood floorboards, the ancestry of which can be traced straight back to the 1940s Volkswagen. Porsche AG probably at some point placed an order for half a million sets of the damn things and felt that it was more economical to use them up than it would have been to switch to molded polyvinylputrate, or whatever.

Porsche is by far the smallest independent mass producer of automobiles on the planet, now that Ferrari is part of Fiat, Rolls-Royce is owned by BMW, Aston Martin by Ford, and Lamborghini, Bugatti, and Bentley belong to VW/Audi. But don't feel sorry for them. Porsche's per-car profit margin has also long been by far the highest in the entire industry. The air-cooled 911 was the most value-added car in the world: a small, simple shell with some elementary suspension at each corner plus an excellent power plant and a lot of leather. (The air-cooled engine is by far the most costly piece of a 911, which is one reason—among several—why Porsche switched to a water-cooled power plant for the current 996 model. A complete new 911 engine, retail, will cost you around $30,000. A complete new 996 engine will cross the dealer's parts counter for about $10,000.)

Another piece of my car that got eighty-sixed was the severely cracked, rhino-hard, leather-covered glareshield above the instrument panel. Porsche, anxious to turn the 911 into a luxury car, apparently realized too late that real leather would never survive the solar heating of the windshield. Or perhaps it doesn't get severely sunny in Germany all that often. After 1984, only vinyl was used on 911 glareshields for the U.S. market, and that's what my brand-new $450 replacement bore. (In 1991, Porsche redesigned the 911 dashboard so that leather could again be used. Maybe they bought better glue.)

Much of the rest of the interior, however—door panels, rear bulkhead, seats, rear side panels, trim—was also leather, and it was in fairly good shape. The front seats were a mistreated mess, the driver's-seat seams split by what I had come to imagine must have been an overweight ignoramus of a previous owner who apparently had a fat ass and huge hands. (The leather of the glareshield over the instruments, directly ahead of the steering wheel, was a lacerated mess where either his pinky rings or hairy knuckles had constantly rubbed against it as he turned the wheel.) But I didn't care: I'd be entirely replacing the seats with new semi-race Recaros anyway.

Ah, the joy of taking things apart. It's so much easier than putting them back together again, as so many young alarm-clock disassemblers have learned.

Chapter Eleven

ACRES OF CARS

Leather is absolutely the wrong material for car seats, never mind that it has become the paradigm of luxury, the de rigueur material for fancy trim-option packages even in economy cars. Leather seats turn into bun-roasters in the sun and icebergs in the cold, and they're the only reason electrically heated seats were ever invented. Worse, leather gives little grip while cornering hard; cloth pants against cloth seats offer a far higher coefficient of friction. Telling that to an upwardly mobile new-car buyer, however, is akin to touting the virtues of paste over diamonds.

But it is nice for areas that one's butt doesn't bless, such as door panels. My car's leather was, however, the light brown of a baby's diarrhea, an unfortunate color that may have looked leathery in the showroom but had weathered to a dirty, pallid sheen. I decided to re-dye it black, for a Darth Vader interior—carpets, instrument panel, glareshield, seats, belts, pedals, leather, sunglasses, briefcase, everything Men In Black.

Well, perhaps a few accents here and there.

Leather is thoroughly dyed during its original manufacture, but it's impossible to replicate this process in a home workshop. There are aftermarket companies that provide paints with which to superficially recolor leather. But these paints can be chipped or scratched off, revealing the original leather color below. You're better off re-coloring your leather with the original shade rather than doing something as drastic as I did in trying to convert light brown to gloss black.

The first step is to condition the leather, because it's probably dried out and needs feeding. Yes, leather eats. Eats oil, mainly, which is why kids used to stroke Neatsfoot Oil into their baseball gloves and mold "the pocket." I haven't touched a baseball glove for half a century, so I'm assuming they're today made of plastic, or perhaps titanium, and no longer dine.

There are a number of compounds on the market with which to do this, and they gently restore some of the leather's softening oils. Don't be tempted to use something like Neatsfoot, though; that's a bit extreme for fine leather. There are plenty of overpriced potions that have been created specifically for people rich and silly enough to treat their cars as art objects.

You perhaps can't imagine, if you're accustomed to buying a $7.95 bottle of Turtle Wax every couple of years, to what lengths the truly committed go in conspicuously consuming car-care products. Zymol "Concours Glaze," for example, costs $176 for an eight-ounce bottle, which would probably shine up a Ferrari—or a Toyota—about once. Each container is "hand-poured," whatever that means, *and* numbered and signed. You—or more likely your manservant—warm up the wax in the palm of your hand before reverently applying it.

But that's not the ultimate. Zymol also sells a wax called Royale, which goes for $5,000 and is delivered in a hand-cut crystal display container. The company says it was originally formulated to preserve the finish of Bugatti Royales. Which is odd, because Royales were all painted with hand-rubbed nitrocellulose lacquer, a paint that has absolutely nothing in common with the two-part urethane enamels generally used on cars today.

There were only seven Royales ever built, between 1929 and 1932, and they were easily the largest passenger cars that ever dented the planet's surface, with four wheels the size of John Deere tractor tires. Big enough, in fact, that when they proved to literally be white elephants, leftover Royale engines were used to power French railroad locomotives. One of them set a world rail speed record of 122 mph in 1934, blowing out all the windows in a variety of train stations through which it passed, much as environmentalists feared the Concorde would do to houses below its flight path.

One day during a travel-magazine assignment that took my twelve-year-old daughter and me to Switzerland, I subjected her to a quick run up the *autoroute* from Basel to Mulhouse, to visit the French National Transportation Museum, still generally referred to as "the Schlumpf Collection." I'd been there once before and, like any motorhead dad, decided this was something my kid needed to see.

— The Schlumpfs were Swiss brothers, owners of a group of huge Alsatian fabric mills, who had a major Bugatti jones. They wanted to own every Bugatti ever made. This wasn't quite possible, but they came close, amassing a collection they put together by buying up every private Bugatti collection they could find. In 1964, American collector John Shakespeare sold his entire collection of 30 Bugattis (including one of the seven Royales) to the Schlumpfs for what was a pittance even then—$85,000—and had them loaded aboard a special freight train and unceremoniously trundled to New Orleans, from whence they were shipped to France.

Four of the seven Royales were in Mulhouse. I asked Brook, more than a decade later, what she remembered of the visit. "Uh, acres of cars?" she said. Not an inaccurate recollection. The Schlumpfs, it turned out, had been using company funds to support their obsession, and finally their workers turned out in an angry horde to put a stop to this deprivation of their pension funds. The brothers' collection, amplified by the addition of hundreds more cars of French manufacture, became France's National Transportation Museum—quite literally "acres of cars," parked row after interminable row in unimaginative chronological order and topical groupings, adhering to some automotive Dewey decimal system.

Royales are the most valuable cars ever made. One reportedly sold at auction for $14 million during the bubble-powered 1990s and thereafter disappeared into Japan. I doubt it's being waxed with Zymol Royale.

I have one catalogue of car-care potions that lists well over 200 products. We're talking basically about car wash, polish, and wax, stuff that in my era was generally lumped under the heading of "Simoniz." Brake-dust remover (and you didn't even know you *had* brake dust), fancy automotive Q-tips, tire "protectant," vinyl and rubber conditioner, battery-terminal spray, brake antisqueal spray (why are brakes suddenly so labor-intensive?), swirl-mark remover, polymer sealant, and both Saab and Volvo Wax but neither Pontiac nor Mercury Wax.

The world of car-care products runs the gamut from useless chemicals—you'll find most of them at any Wal-Mart—to perfectly useful ones that are ludicrously overpriced. At one end of the spectrum are liquids and sprays that use the extremely temporary but briefly dazzling effect of cheap silicone on vinyl, rubber, and paint to make rubes imagine they have actually "polished" their car by simply wiping it with a wetted cloth. At the other end are wares that are basically carnauba—made from the oil of a Brazilian nut—which is a superb wax for paint but is really no better when it costs $200 than when it costs $20. (Butcher's furniture wax is an excellent carnauba wax, but don't put it on your car.)

But we were talking about leather, weren't we?

Right.

After you have the leather reasonably happy and pliable again, the next step is to seriously mistreat it. You drench it with quick-drying lacquer thinner and then distress it with scrapers and sandpaper to remove as much as possible of the old surface color coating. The paint that's on the leather is what seriously stiffens it and helps to form cracks, and you need to remove as much of it as possible, through a combination of softening it with the thinner and then beating it up it with whatever floats your boat—steel wool, Scotchbrite, medium-coarse sandpaper, scraper blades, razors, an old jackknife, or whatever. Don't be shy. Leather is tough stuff, else cattle wouldn't wear it.

If you work at it over and over again, you should be able to get at least 80 percent of the old coloring off, which is necessary to provide a good footing for the new paint. The dye can then be applied—once the leather is dry—with a soft-haired brush. Which is what I did, but if I had it to do over again, I'd spray it on with a good trim-size paint gun. The brush marks show, albeit only slightly if you're careful, and there are the inevitable stray brush-hairs that become a permanent part of your new interior once the leather paint has dried.

What am I saying, "If I had it to do over again"? Once the car is finished, I'm going to go back and start correcting all the things I've done wrong.

Chapter Twelve

PAUL THE NEWFIE

B ut then some of the things I've done wrong I can't correct, and
don't even want to. Like my foray into the scary world of serious
dope smuggling.

My friend Bob Hoffman was one of the few hipsters in the aviation
world in the late 1960s—a time when flying private planes was something done by Middle Americans, many of whom had either taken part
in World War II, wished they'd been old enough to, or, like Ronald Rea-
gan, imagined they had. It was appropriate that the capital of the lightplane industry was Wichita, Kansas, smack in the middle of the heartland
of the Silent Majority.

Hoffman, a hippie-dippie aviation writer-editor, former flight instructor, and part-time folksinger-guitarist, bartender, and ski instructor,
had a bellowing Bahstun accent and an easy laugh, both of which came
roaring out of his skinny frame. (His nickname around the office was
Screech.) Hoffman was the bane of "Captain Eddie" Muhlfeld, the gruff,
pompous man who ran the two aviation magazines for which Bob and I
then worked—*Flying* in my case and the even straighter *Business & Com-
mercial Aviation* in Hoffman's.

Both were Ziff-Davis magazines. ZD was one of those rare companies built to moderate proportions by a father and then made hugely
successful by a visionary son—in this case the then-young Bill Ziff. The

elder Ziff and his long-forgotten partner Bernard Davis found a small measure of fortune in the 1930s and 1940s publishing fantasy and science-fiction magazines of the sort that featured on their covers what were then referred to as BEMs (bug-eyed monsters) and would today be called ETs. But when "young Bill" took over the company on his father's death in 1956, he set about inventing the big-time specialty magazine—hobbyist monthlies catering to car enthusiasts, private pilots, amateur photographers, skiers, boaters, hi-fi nuts, and the like.

It was the mid-1960s, and I'd been working at a glamorous (but now also long-forgotten) travel magazine called *Holiday*. It was still the time of big, broad-based general-interest magazines—the *Saturday Evening Post, Life, Look*—but I'd learned to fly and gotten my pilot's license, and I thought it would be fun to play with and write about airplanes. So I quit *Holiday* and signed on at Ziff-Davis's *Flying,* which in the Manhattan publishing world then was akin to today going from Condé Nast to *Cat Fancy.* Yet somehow, I had stumbled onto the beginning-to-boom world of special-interest magazines, neatly stepping ashore from one of the sinking leviathans that until then had dominated magazine publishing. *Holiday* folded a couple of years later.

Hoffman didn't last long at *B/CA,* which was a trade magazine for corporate pilots and bizjet salesmen—very straight people who wore white shirts and white belts and called Martinis see-throughs. Bob was anything but straight. He and I were what the straights called longhairs, which was a bad thing to be in the airplane business in the days when Vietnam was the country's preoccupation. Most professional pilots had come out of the military, and the only difference between them and most private pilots was that the amateurs *wished* they'd been in the Air Force.

I lost track of Hoffman, but then a good ten years later, out of nowhere—well, Florida, actually—he called me.

He needed a pilot. Somebody with a fair amount of multi-engine time and the ability to fly a big Cessna 402. In fact, Hoffman needed a multi-engine pilot who wanted to do some drug smuggling.

It wasn't the first time I'd been asked. A couple of years earlier, my actor/bartender friend Gino Dante—OK, Gene Mekler, but Gino Dante was his stage name—had put me together with a scary Israeli, a former Mossad guy, who was running an enormous dope-smuggling business.

How enormous? My then-girlfriend/now-wife and I went to dinner at his Greenwich Village apartment, where after coffee he showed us his "operations center." Behind a straight-out-of-the-movies revolving section of bookshelves lay a dim, low-ceilinged, garretlike room. A dozen automatic weapons were racked on one wall—everything from long-magazined machine pistols to Kalashnikovs—and arrayed along another were short-wave radios, softly babbling, seemingly to each other. (This was the early 1970s, when communication involved Hallicrafters that looked like oscilloscopes and Motorola two-ways, not PCs and Nokias.)

The man told us he did most of his smuggling by boat—hence the ship-to-shore radios—but what he really wanted was for me to find a Boeing 707 to fly for him. Mexico, he explained, had built a number of jet-length runways in remote areas in anticipation of a tourist boom that never went off, and he had made a deal with the *federales* who controlled one of them. This was before anybody in the U.S. could do much about airborne smugglers other than occasionally briefly track them on radar.

I could fly in and out with impunity, hauling tons and tons of marijuana under well-paid Mexican police protection each time.

I explained to him that I really wasn't competent to fly a 707, but thanks for the thought. What Susan remembers best is that he pressed upon us a large shopping bag filled with fragrant, unprocessed marijuana—twigs and seeds, largely. It was a small honorarium for my time. We kept trying to mislay it, not quite sure how to hit the crowded Manhattan streets lugging a grocery bag of grass, but my new smuggler friend saw us out the door. "Here, don't forget this," he said.

It took us two years to smoke a little of it and give away the rest.

Hoffman was different. I was perhaps the only person more naïve about smuggling than he was. Bob moved in some strange Miami circles, and he had somehow fallen in with a young ex-Newfoundlander who trafficked mainly in marijuana, sometimes from Florida, sometimes LA, and sometimes Canada. "Me grandfather was a smoogler, me father was a smoogler, and I'm a smoogler too," Paul the Newfie explained to me when I met him. He was simply going into the family business, having grown up on an island that had specialized in the trade back when liquor and cigarettes were the commodities of choice.

I had long assumed that pot was a recreational drug used by jazz musicians, tie-dyed collegians, and hip Manhattanites, but Paul knew that an entire generation of men had come back from Vietnam permanently stoned, and many of them had gone to work in factories or home to ghettos. His destinations weren't Greenwich Village, Ann Arbor, and Cambridge, they were places like Flint, Michigan, and Bridgeport, Connecticut—factory towns and blasted heaths, some that had been taken over largely by minority populations. Drugs were the only thing that had gotten these people through the war, and they were the only thing that made working on an assembly line bearable. Paul's market was hard-core, not people like me who occasionally played at getting high. I was in *way* over my head.

Marijuana is bulky, and Paul had been shipping it hither and yon in U-Haul box trucks filled with packed-tight cartons of weed hidden just forward of a thin camouflage layer of random furniture and household goods. The vans were driven by young couples, like Hoffman and his girlfriend—attractive, harmless twosomes in their thirties who looked like they had every reason to be moving from Miami to Seattle, which happened to be one run Bob had recently done for the Newfie. Each van was followed, a half mile behind, by a car bearing a couple of Paul's confederates, just to make sure the mules didn't get any ideas.

On one trip, another chauffeuring young couple had stopped at a highway pull-off in Wyoming to change drivers and relax their stretched-tight nerves. A Highway Patrol car pulled in behind them, the cop simply wanting a stretch himself. But the box-truck driver, immediately assuming the jig was up, did an immediate hands-up and was about to assume the brace position alongside the truck. It only took a few seconds for the trooper to see that something wasn't right. The Newfie sedan glided past, saying goodbye to one more load.

"We need an airplane," Paul said, "and somebody reliable to fly it." He meant stupid enough to fly it. That would be me.

Hoffman obtained the airplane, spending about $100,000 of Paul's unmarked $100 bills on a well-used twelve-seat Cessna twin of a size in those days normally employed as a small commuter liner. Bob was delighted to be the owner of record, a move that would later prove awkward: California, to which he'd moved and where he'd registered the airplane, eventually came after him to pay the sales tax, which roughly equaled his annual take as a bartender. Hoffman eventually got out of it by moving to an all but nameless Caribbean island where he became the editor/ reporter/photographer/compositor/ad salesman of the local newspaper.

Despite the fact that Susan had become my wife and we had a six-month-old baby, I was unable to resist whatever presented itself as the thrill ride of the moment, particularly when it provided me with a big, fancy airplane to fly and there were hints that it would make me lots of money. So I flew off to California to meet Paul the Newfie and accept employment as his new "corporate pilot." In a furnitureless house in the San Fernando Valley, its windows so heavily draped it was night at noon, strange young women glided hither and yon while Paul peeled five $100 bills off a wad the size of a hockey puck and gave them to me as walking-around money for the next few days. "And get your hair cut," he said. My hirsute New York freelancer look was a little too out-there for him.

Hoffman and I sat around his little North Hollywood cottage for what seemed like forever before getting the call from Paul to scramble the 402 for our first mission: a flight from LA to Flint, Michigan, site of a big ancient, rough-and-tumble Buick factory. Why we were going there empty I have no idea. Unless we in fact weren't empty.

Certainly the cabin was, but the 402 had a voluminous baggage compartment in its Roman nose, and perhaps Paul's people had secreted something up there. Never mind, that fit right in with the defense I had planned to call upon if we were ever caught: "I'm just the pilot. You don't arrest the cabbie because his passenger has a pocketful of cocaine, right?" My sister-in-law, a Chicago lawyer of note, looked at me in stark horror when I detailed this brilliant legal strategy to her.

My most vivid memory of the trip east to Flint was crossing the Rockies at night in a big, unpressurized airplane, sucking oxygen through a mask. I looked not down but across at floodlit resort skiers. In the dark, the Cessna's turbochargers glowed bright red through the cooling gills atop each nacelle, from the exhaust heat coursing through them. Sobering to think how close they were to the melting point of iron.

We parked the 402 in a hangar at the Flint airport, where it stayed for weeks, and I flew home on an airliner. Susan picked me up at LaGuardia, baby Brook in her arms. As soon as we got into the car, I snapped open my little suitcase and showed her my pay for the trip—$3,000 in small bills, which at that point in my freelance-writing career was equivalent to ten magazine articles. "Yeah, very nice," Susan said. She had spent three weeks wondering whether Brook would next converse with me through a plate-glass visiting-room window at Riker's Island. We kept the $3,000 in the freezer, chipping off bunches of bills as the need arose.

There were occasional 2:00 A.M. telephone calls from Paulie. "Can you come up to Toronto right away, eh?" "Say, we got a van full of weed that broke down in Arizona. Can you run out and pick up its load, eh?" Fortunately, they either came during blizzards or when I didn't yet have the right aeronautical charts for the route. Paul didn't seem to much care.

Two weeks later, I went back to miserable, depressed, weary Flint and retrieved the 402. On the flight back to New York, half the systems in the airplane eventually failed as the poor old thing decided enough was enough. Paul told Hoffman to get rid of it; he'd figure something else out. (At least he had finally realized that he was dealing with two total amateurs, no matter how well we could fly an airplane.) I flew the 402 to a used-airplane broker in Atlanta and came home on an airline. The next day, the broker called and said the left engine was on the verge of failure, several of its cylinders registering zero compression. "Oh, and it looks like you might have had a fire back in the turbocharger section on that side. Lucky the fire must have blown out."

Lucky indeed. The things we do for a thrill, the things we get away with heedlessly, the stupidities we commit for the fun of it. Does everybody do this, or is it just me?

Chapter Thirteen

BLACK & DECKER TIME

A 911's dashboard gauges can easily be removed. Try it on your Ford Explorer or Toyota Camry and you'll find that pretty much the whole dashboard has to come out. But each 911 instrument is separate, a round metal soup-can pressed into a matching hole on the dash. All that holds it in place is a rubber gasket just behind the decorative bezel around the instrument face. To pull a 911 gauge out, just sit in the driver's seat and pry it toward you—with your fingernails if they're strong or otherwise any small, flat tool that can be inserted between bezel and dashboard. An ordinary table knife works just fine.

One crucial, continual act during the dismantling of a car is making notes and diagrams anytime you take apart something that will need to be reassembled in a not particularly intuitive way. The back of each gauge, for example, is a thicket of color-coded wires leading to spade connectors, sockets, and plugs. Some are for ordinary night-lighting bulbs, some are the drivers for such crucial indicators as oil pressure, and some are plain old ground wires. On combination gauges—the ones that indicate several parameters on one dial—there can be a dozen or so wires. Mix them up at your peril. Obviously, a shop-manual wiring diagram can ultimately be used to correct mistakes, but it's far simpler to keep a notepad filled with such things as physical diagrams of the gauge connectors.

Easy access to a 911's gauges also means that since the speedo-meter can be removed by a twelve-year-old or a former Harvard English major—who occasionally share the same mechanical acuity—the potential for odometer-tampering is considerable. And indeed, my speedo showed the unmistakable, telltale marks of having been opened. Arrgh. Had I bought what I thought was a mid-mileage car that had actually driven to the moon and back? Damn. Why am I surprised, having shopped at that sleazy Long Island City warehouse?

Speedometers and other 911 VDO gauges are sealed with a metal bezel—the same one you pry against to get the gauge out of the dash—that holds the face glass in place against the instrument. The bezel is pressed in place by a rotating tool that zips around its periphery and smoothly flares the malleable metal band against the instrument case. But that thin bezel can just as easily be removed simply by prying its backside up with a small screwdriver or a knife tip.

That provides instant access to the odometer, and then it's the flick of a finger to change a 289,000 mileage total to 89,000, which could conceivably have been the case with the car I bought. The telltale signs: though the bezel can easily be resealed by tap-tap-tapping around its circumference with a small hammer and punch, it'll never again show the smooth surface of a wheel-sealed gauge. Mine had obviously been opened and resealed manually.

Ultimately, it didn't much matter to me, since I was intent on replac-ing just about every moving part of the car anyway. But if you're ever shopping for a used 911, pull the speedo out of the panel and look for signs of bezel-tampering—a slightly ripply, manipulated look where the back of the bezel seals against the instrument case.

There are two reasons why a 911 speedometer might have been opened. One, obviously, is to have turned the odometer back and con-verted a commuter-trashed beater into a low-mileage, driven-only-on-sunny-weekends sweetheart.

The other is because somebody quite legitimately needed to replace the plastic odometer-drive gear, which is a common failure in vintage 911s. Trying to zero the trip meter while the car is in motion can fail the gear, and it's one of those things learned only through experience, since there's no warning in the owner's manual. If the seller can show you a shop receipt or logbook record confirming odometer repair, you're reasonably safe . . . though who can doubt that some do-it-yourselfers could repair the gear and be unable to resist the temptation to then turn the odometer back as well.

A confession, now that the statute of limitations has expired and the airplane lives in Melbourne, Australia: When I built that airplane—my pre-Porsche project—the FAA required of me forty hours of no-passengers/no-destination test-flying, never straying more than twenty-five miles from my home airport. After that was done and duly logged, the Feds would sign off the airplane and grant its official Certificate of Airworthiness. Forty hours was twice the length of time I should by regulations have been required to spend at the task, and the reason for the doubling was a silly bit of bureaucratic stubbornness too stupid to bother recounting.

But forty hours of flying . . . wow, that added up to $4,300 worth of pointless-to-pointless aviating, in terms of avgas, expensive and frequently changed oil, wear and tear, and other typically overpriced aeronautical delights. And I knew it really wasn't necessary. After twenty hours of proof testing, I knew the airplane's wings wouldn't fall off and its engine wouldn't stop. I was sure of that, else I wouldn't have continued to fly the thing.

So what did I do? A hint is that it's called "logging Black & Decker time."

A light airplane's tachometer, which reads the engine's revolutions per minute (rpm), also contains an odometer-like, spooling-numbers, total-time accumulator called an hour meter. The hour meter is the official record of how many hours and tenths of hours the airplane has been in operation—flight time plus everything that happens on the ground while the engine is running, which is mainly taxiing to and from the runway.

Though a Porsche's speedometer and tachometer are driven electrically, through small wires, a light airplane's tach is run the old-fashioned way, entirely mechanically, by a flexible cable the size of a thick pencil lead that stretches from the engine through the firewall to the back of the tachometer, inside a protective sheath. So I unscrewed the cable from the engine, attached an electric drill to it—hence "Black & Decker time"—and turned the drill on full speed. In an hour or so, the little digits on the face of the tach had advanced from 0020.00 to 0040.00.

So sue me.

Actual automotive odometer-tampering is in fact a felony—a serious Federal as well as state crime with enormous fines and even hard time, particularly for those used-car dealers who routinely do it for a living and occasionally get caught. It goes on constantly, especially in a time when buyers are looking for slightly used—the politically correct term is "pre-owned"—cars with low mileage.

It's the reason why the old-fashioned, easily altered, revolving-drum mechanical odometer has all but disappeared, replaced by electronic odos that read out in LED numerals. But the bad guys have figured out how to beat them as well—I assume with devices that transmit signals to recon-figure the glowing-numerals readout. A little Internet research will find you places to take your car where for $200 they'll make the mileage read anything your cheatin' heart desires.

My Porsche's odometer currently is counting up from zero. When I finally put the 911 back on the road, it was with fat 245/45-16 tires on eight-inch-wide wheels in place of the original 225s on sevens, so I sent the speedo to a highly regarded Porsche-instrument repair shop to have it recalibrated for the changed rolling diameter of the rear wheels. "While you're at it," I told them, "turn the odo back to zero. The car's all new, so let's start the clock over again."

Yet the speedo would prove to be one of the most truculent parts of the car, once I finally got it back on the road. I *know* it was working when I bought the battered original SC, since I'd surely have noticed a dead needle, but now not only the odometer but also the speed read zero. Back to the shop the speedometer went for an overhaul. Back into the car, hooked up the mass of wires, turned on the key . . . oh, shit, why is it read-ing 180 mph? Because I'd hooked up two of the wires backward, that's why. Blew a diode. Back to the shop, back into the car, off for a drive . . . still zero.

A 911SC's speedometer is driven by a little round sensor that clips to the outside of the transmission. Inside that sensor, a tiny microswitch snaps closed every time a magnet on the differential's ring gear rotates past. Since the rotational speed of the ring gear is exactly equivalent to the speed at which the rear wheels are turning, the speedometer counts how rapidly the magnet is momentarily closing the switch and moves the speedo needle the equivalent amount.

Okay, must be a bad sensor. Bought a new one—$70—and installed it. Nothing. A knowledgeable friend told me, "Check it with a multimeter. You should get continuity through the two wires." No continuity, so it went back to the supplier with an angry note and I tried a *third* sensor. Didn't work either. Checked all the wiring. It was fine. Found out my friend was wrong, you only get an indication of sensor continuity if you hold a magnet against it, closing the switch. Tried that, and, of course, both the new sensor and the one that had originally been on the car worked just fine. I'd been through three perfectly good units.

Wait a minute. I *know* that it's possible to put the sensor against the transmission backward, somebody already warned me about that, but obviously the potted, raw-looking side of the little cylinder goes against the gearbox and the finished metal side faces outward, right?

Wrong: I'd spent a month trying to troubleshoot a perfectly good speedo with the sensor on backward.

Sometimes, it's the little things that get you.

Chapter Fourteen

SHE FALLS TO PIECES

Most of a 911 comes apart easily. It's a matter of undoing bolts and nuts, and quickly the car becomes a shell. A Porsche 911 is a surprisingly simple car. I say "surprisingly" because this machine is treated with such reverence by many admirers largely because they assume it's complex and exotic. It is actually a stunningly simple design.

The air-cooled 911 was introduced in 1963. It remained in production, unchanged except for details—OK, some of them pretty major, such as an engine that grew from 2.0 liters to 3.6—*(www.rennsport systems.com)* until 1989. Twenty-six years. Most cars are totally redesigned and re-engineered every five years. Some models live as long as ten years, typically because they're from a company such as Saab or Land Rover that can't afford to play the new-new-entirely-new game every half-decade.

In fact, there has never been an automobile model that survived true to its basic design as long as the 911 did. Not the Model T, not the VW Bug, not the Fiat Cinquecento, or anything else on wheels. Whatever else you want to say in criticism of the 911, this was one majorly workable, usable, utilitarian design. The 911's shape, rear-engine configuration, and nomenclature endure to this day. It's still called "a 911," though the current water-cooled car doesn't have a single part in common with mine. Porsche has even design-patented the basic turtleback-coupe shape.

A few weeks' work—a real mechanic could have done it in days—reduced my little red 911 to a single chunk of sheet metal that I could lift off the four jack stands on which it sat. Not all four at once, but I could get a grip on the nose or tail of what remained and lever it up and down as though I were Andre the Giant.

A 911 can quickly be reduced—using household tools, as the TV ad would put it—to its floorpan platform plus the pieces welded to it: the rear fenders and tail, the engine-compartment firewall, the roof, the door openings and windshield pillars, the sheet metal of the instrument panel and front bulkhead, and the wedge-shaped front trunk area. (The windshield, rear window, and side windows all pop right out, and the two voluptuous front fenders entirely unbolt from the rest of the body.) And what I was left with was the shell of a car that sat in the barn looking like every Porsche owner's nightmare of what would happen to a 911 abandoned overnight on the Cross-Bronx Expressway if Tom Hanks had been driving it instead of a Mercedes-Benz in *Bonfire of the Vanities.*

I shouldn't condescend. When I worked for *Car and Driver* in the mid-1970s, we kept our constant flow of manufacturer-provided test cars in the Red Ball, a scruffy Manhattan parking garage on East Thirty-First Street. In and out constantly, we editors became what we imagined to be quasibuddies of the hard guys who ran the place. They were mainly unsmiling kids in do-rags and impenetrable sunglasses. But they loved our new test-car GTOs and Caddies, the Alfa-Romeos and Jaguars.

Coming back to the Red Ball late one night in some nameless Corinthian-leathered Chrysler, the epitome of Detroit shoddiness and Iacoccan bad taste, I mentioned to Carlos as I dropped it off, "Hey, just saw some dude parked a broken-down new Saab up on the Harlem River Drive."

It was as though I'd wandered onto an RAF aerodrome in September 1940 and said, "Hey, just saw some Heinkel 111s heading this way." After a microsecond of stunned silence, six young Puerto Ricans somehow piled into a turbocharged and lowered four-seat Volkswagen Rabbit and took off like a scrambled Spitfire.

I have no doubt that the next morning, some suburban commuter came back to find his new Saab sitting on four milk crates, the wheels, tires, and much of the interior gone.

I could have used the help of Carlos and his crew. Some of my bolts and nuts required persuasion, having been in place for seventeen years, frozen there by the actions of corrosion, road chemicals, time, and simple mechanical obstinance.

The Great Persuader is heat. Heat from a propane gun sometimes is enough, but serious heat from a welding torch is the next step. Especially heat in combination with a good antiseize fluid, known generically as mouse milk. Forget the ordinary hardware-store Liquid Wrench and find a good, carcinogenic, paint-eating professional product. Ask any local pro mechanic his preference and use it.

Hit the chosen fastener with heat, wait till it cools just enough to not vaporize the liquid, spray it with mouse milk, and let the liquid wick into the tortured, expanding/contracting joint. Wait a few hours, do it again if necessary, hit the bastard with a torch once more, and guaranteed it'll give in to the force of a good six-point socket on a breaker bar. Of course, I was fortunate that I didn't burn down the barn during all these pyrotechnics.

Leverage is the key. A nut that will never give in to a puny little eight-inch-long ratchet handle will fall easily to an eighteen-inch breaker bar. Either that or the stud—or the tool—will shear. One big advantage of Sears Craftsman tools is that though they're of excellent quality (though not the Snap-On/Facom ultimate), if you break anything, their lifetime guarantee means the tool is replaced no questions asked. Often it's easier to do that by running down to your local Sears than it is to find a Snap-On dealer. The only exception to this policy, not surprisingly, is three-eighths-to-half-inch socket-wrench adapters: given the leverage of a half-inch-socket breaker bar working an ordinary three-eighths socket through such an adapter, a twelve-year-old can shear the adapter.

By the time I was done disassembling, I'd removed . . .
- the entire interior
- the wheel hubs, brakes, and brake lines

- the complete front and rear suspension, including the two torsion bars that run across the car
- the two rear axles and their CV (constant velocity) joints
- the big gas tank in the trunk
- all of the glass including the windshield
- the front fenders and both doors
- the oil tank in the right rear fender plus the oil lines and oil cooler in the right front fender
- the complex, archaic, semi-useless air-conditioning system and all its plumbing
- all of the mechanisms such as the windshield-wiper motor and air blower in the trunk
- and last, but hardly least, the entire engine/transmission unit.

Chapter Fifteen

FALCO

T he Porsche was not my first big do-it-yourself project. I'd already built that airplane.

When I tell people I've built an airplane, some say, "Oh, cool. I used to build model airplanes, too." No, I explain, this airplane was one-to-one scale. Life-size.

"You could *sit* in it?"

Actually, two people could sit in it.

"An ultralight, right?"

No, not one of those parasol-wing things built with lawn-furniture hardware and a chain-saw engine, my airplane was a serious traveling machine. Serious enough that when I sold it to a man who moved to Australia, he had a professional pilot ferry it all the way from the U.S. to Melbourne via Europe and the Middle East, in one of the longest flights ever made by an amateur-built airplane.

The airplane that I built in my barn was an Italian design that in the 1960s had been manufactured by a series of Italian companies that saw it as the perfect plaything for wealthy Eurosporties with pilots' licenses. Called the Falco, it was quite fast and very beautiful. So it was inevitably dubbed "the Ferrari of the air." It helped that most were red.

Yet under the red paint was not a Ferrari's aluminum but wood. The Falco was made of aviation-grade Alaskan Sitka spruce—some of the purest, straightest, most flawless and lightest wood in the world—and fine Scandinavian birch plywood. It had been designed to be built by cottage industry in a country still crawling out from under World War II. Early semifinished Falcos were taken from the factory, in Milan, to the airport on horse-drawn carts to be assembled and test flown, presumably while the horses watched. If Italian carpenters who drank wine with lunch could build one, I figured so could I.

The Falco was unknown in the U.S. until a wealthy, eccentric, endlessly voluble Virginian pilot named Alfred Scott—Scott Stadium at the University of Virginia is named for his grandfather—was captivated by the design, which he saw only in a coffee-table airplane book. He somehow persuaded its designer, Stelio Frati, to allow him to turn the impossibly complex factory-built Falco into a kit that American do-it-themselfers could build.

He must have caught Frati unawares, because the notoriously crusty aeronautical engineer—trust me, I've been the object of Frati's famous wrath for things I've written about his airplanes—agreed to let this unknown Southerner convert his dog-eared old, rolled-up-in-a-rug Italian blueprints into clean, comparatively simple American plans that eventually were computer-generated. To find suppliers who would turn out multiples of every unique aluminum bell crank and bracket, fitting and fixture on the Falco. And to contract with a professional cabinetmaker to laminate, clamp, bend, and glue together all the basic wooden structures that formed a Falco so that they could be sold as components of an aircraft-building kit.

I admire people like Alfred Scott, but I don't know many of them. People who have the sheer determination to say, "OK, I can do this. I'm not sure how, but how hard can it be?" Well, Scott assumedly was at least an aeronautical engineer, right?

Alfred, bless his heart, graduated from the University of Virginia as a drama major, became a folk singer, and before he began the Falco project owned a string of gas stations.

We had a great deal in common. Mostly that neither of us ever knew, or cared, what we were getting into before starting a project. I think we both subscribed to the Confucian doctrine that the longest journey is merely a series of individual footsteps.

Still, there are few things as sensual to me as a box of parts. "Stop me before I kit again," I think to myself every time I tear the shrink-wrap off one of the scale-model kits I to this day continue to build: 1:48-scale airplanes of painstaking detail, each ultimately airbrushed in dead-accurate color and supplied with decals some so small they require a loupe to read. But nothing can compare to the box of parts that is a modern, full-size kitplane such as a Falco.

Actually, it was dozens of boxes, ranging from six-pack-size sets of electronics fittings to the carton the length of a small sailboat's mast that held the making of the airplane's main wing spar. Nor was it a matter of simply "assembling" the kit in an "insert-tab-A-in-slot-B" fashion. Everything that required complex machining or welding—landing gear, gas tanks, engine mount, and the like—had been prefabbed. Everything that required steam bending and laminating of wood—fuselage frames and spars—was also done. But there was lots left to do.

I spent five years, $83,000, and uncounted man-hours building the Falco. The all-wood airframe was literally glued together with an unusual powdered adhesive called Aerolite. When the white powder was mixed with water, it produced a sticky goop that I couldn't help but realize looked exactly like semen.

Whatever it resembled, Aerolite had an honorable history. During World War II, the British company de Havilland designed an all-wood airplane called the Mosquito, and Aerolite was invented to glue Mosquitoes together. Made much the same way the Falco was, of spruce and plywood, Mosquitoes were intended to conserve valuable aluminum and be built by subcontractors who'd previously been making furniture or fiddles rather than airplanes.

The Mosquito, powered by two massive Rolls-Royce Merlin V12 engines, was one of the fastest airplanes of the war. So fast that it was frequently used as a photoreconnaissance airplane, sent over enemy territory to take pictures of targets. There were no guns aboard photorecon Mossies, because the Germans had no airplanes capable of catching one.

When I finished my Falco, I continued the military theme by painting it in Italian air force colors—implement gray with bright-red nose, tail, and wing tips. The red I used, quite coincidentally, was Porsche Guards Red—the exact original color of the 911 that was still in my future.

That *Aeronautica Militare Italiano* color scheme, with red, white, and green roundels on the fuselage, was phony. No Falco ever flew with the Italian air force. But the Falco's look-alike successor, the more powerful, all metal SF-260 that Stelio Frati designed for the Italian company SIAI-Marchetti, did. The SF-260 also flew for Burma, the Congo, Libya, and many other third-world countries. I have a friend who bought an ex-Congolese SF-260 that he swears had a hole in its fuselage made by a spear, and at one time, Muammar Qadhafi owned the world's largest collection of aircraft designed by Stelio Frati—several dozen SF-260s.

One of the first people to complete a kit-built Falco was David Aronson, a middle-aged insurance executive from Minnesota. He had quietly created such a lovely, smooth, glossy, compulsive, perfect airplane that I made plans to meet him at a big air show in Florida, where my in-laws lived. I planned to write an aviation-magazine article about his Falco. It would also be a good excuse for my wife and daughter and me to travel to the grandparents in the airplane that we owned while I was building our Falco. It was a classic, high-performance Piper Comanche single-engine retractable. Not so fast as my Falco would be, but a four-seater. ("We're a family of three," my wife would occasionally point out. "Why are we building a two-seat airplane? So one of us will survive?")

The Minnesotan and I were southbound toward Florida at the same time. He was coming from Minneapolis with a fellow-pilot friend. We were heading downrange from New York. Susan, Brook, and I got as far as Jacksonville, where a line of huge Florida thunderstorms loomed.

Thunderstorms are many a pilot's deepest and most intractable fear. Each full-grown boomer encompasses pretty much the energy of a nuclear explosion. An expertly flown airplane, even a small one, can survive a thunderstorm. I've done it several times, never want to again, and wish I hadn't tried it then. I saw colors inside those storms that I didn't know existed in nature and been frightened till I almost wet my pants. The vaunted "hurricane hunters," the big Air Force and Navy turboprops that deliberately fly into hurricanes to keep track of their growth, have a far easier job than does a light-plane pilot who blunders into a thunderhead. Thunderstorms occasionally knock down airliners.

But we stopped at JAX, racing the storms to the airport, battling our way down the ILS—the instrument landing system—and touching down while rain swept the tarmac. (What kind of idiot does this to a wife and child? You tell me.) We waited for several hours while the storms passed through, then continued to Naples.

"Your friend just crashed and killed himself," my father-in-law said as we walked in the door of their condo. Irwin had a strange sense of humor, so I thought he was kidding. "No, somebody named Alfred Scott just called and said your guy crashed somewhere upstate."

David Aronson had run into part of the same weather system we had, but it was dark by the time he reached it. And he was low on fuel. He tried a "back-course" instrument approach to the airport at Gainesville, Florida, failed to find the runway, went back to try a second time, and ran out of fuel during the attempt.

A conventional full-ILS approach to a runway in bad weather is pretty easy to fly. A round dial on the airplane's panel has two long indicator needles. One floats up and down, the other left and right. Radio beams from transmitters aligned with the runway activate the needles. To fly in a gentle descent to the runway in bad weather, when there's nothing to see through the windscreen but cloud and rain, you control the airplane so that the up-down needle stays absolutely centered. To fly such a descent while perfectly aligned with the runway centerline, you simultaneously control the airplane so the left-right needle is also centered. The instrument will show a perfect cross, like a sinner's fingers making a get-thee-behind-me-Satan symbol.

Centering the needles simply requires the pilot to fly "toward" them. If the horizontal glide-slope needle begins to rise, you slow the airplane's rate of descent until the needle begins to back down to the center of the gauge. If the vertical left-right needle begins to drift to the right, you turn slightly to the right, toward it, until it re-centers.

The problem with back-course approaches is that for one thing, there is no altitude guidance. The radio beam that defines the glide slope is at the other end of the runway, pointing in the other direction, and can't be used. Descending to the runway at the proper angle requires some mental arithmetic based on the airplane's ground speed, altitude at the beginning of the approach, and the distance to the runway.

That's in fact easier than it sounds, thanks to precomputed tables printed on the approach plate—the minimap that shows every parameter of an instrument approach. The real problem for some pilots is that though the localizer beam—the one that works the left-right needle and defines the centerline of the runway—is perfectly usable, since it points in both directions down the runway, a back-course approach requires that you fly *away* from the needle to correct your course. Imagine driving a car and suddenly entering a stretch of highway upon which you had to turn the wheel to the right to steer left.

The radar traces of Aronson's two approaches show squiggly back-and-forth bracketing of the localizer beam, like a beagle running left and then right, trying desperately to find the scent. In this case, Aronson apparently never did. Trying to fly an airplane that had suddenly become a glider, at night, in bad weather, proved too difficult. The Falco stalled and then spun heavily to the ground, killing both men instantly.

Small airplanes can be dangerous. From that night on, there were occasional but inevitable moments when, as I sanded and glued, fitted and bolted my Falco together, I wondered whether I was lovingly crafting the instrument of my own doom.

Chapter Sixteen

"THAT AIN'T A PORSCHE, IT'S A FERRARI"

The indelicate act of removing a car's power plant is usually referred to as "pulling the engine," which in most cases is literally true: you take off the hood, unbolt whatever is holding the engine into the car, attach a chain hoist, and pull it up and out of the engine compartment. Shade-tree mechanics are called that not because they want to work out of the sun, but because they need a fat tree-limb to attach the hoist to so they can pull the engine in the backyard, amid old refrigerators and rusty bicycles.

Not in a Porsche, however. The engine is like a fat man in a phone booth. It would never fit through the little hatch at the back of the car that you open to check the oil.

In a 911, you "drop" the engine. A 911's engine/transmission unit comes out of the car from below. In fact, a classic piece of how-to-remove-a-911-engine advice is:

1. Jack the rear of the car way up in the air.
2. Slide a mattress under it.
3. Undo the axles from the gearbox and the four big engine and transmission mounting bolts.
4. Stand back.

WHOOOOMP! The engine will fall onto the mattress, and the dozens of wires, hoses, cables, tubes, pipes, and connectors attached to the engine will all tear loose, thus saving you the job of laboriously finding and freeing each of them.

Kidding, just kidding. . .

Truth to tell, there are few professional Porsche mechanics who haven't lowered an engine out of a 911 without sometime, somewhere forgetting to first disconnect something, whether it's the wire to the backup-light switch on the transmission or the vacuum hose that leads to the brake booster.

Part of my stubborn pride was doing the restoration job in primitive surroundings. My shop was the mid-nineteenth century barn that had once housed three cows, as far as I could tell, or perhaps two cows and a draft horse. Probably some chickens, too, plus a hayloft to help see the brutes through the harsh Hudson Valley winters. The floor was thick-planked and nubbled with thousands of hoof-dents, and there were cracks here and there that, before I was through with the Porsche, would swallow a variety of small but expensive tools and parts. I made no effort to retrieve them, having once watched a five-foot-long Eastern diamond-back rattlesnake lazily slither toward its nest under the barn through a chink in the rubble foundation.

It would be the barn's last hurrah. One corner was crumbling. I'd temporarily shored it up with a grid of two-by-fours so at least it wouldn't collapse on the car. The roof leaked in places, and in a corner stall, the floor had collapsed completely, probably from a combination of groundwater and generations of cow piss.

Several months after finishing the Porsche, I met a barn conservator at a local party. He came to look at the structure and insisted it simply *had* to be restored, the lovely old thing.

An Upstate New York barn-restoration company sent an appraiser. "Sure, we can do it," he said after prodding and measuring, climbing and crawling. "But you'd be crazy. It'd cost you $40,000, and all you'd end up with is an old barn that'd last another twenty or forty years. For that kind of money, you could build a brand-new barn."

Which is exactly what I did, for just under $34,000. My barn-conservator friend will never forgive me.

It would be fun to someday restore a car in a four-bay, flat-floored, polyurethane-coated Southern California garage with a refrigerator full of Corona beer and a bunch of wheeled Facom tool cabinets to glide hither and yon. But for me, it'll never happen. I can't abide neighbors and have always said I need to live far enough in the woods that I can pee off my porch, which I indeed do.

A classic Porsche joke: Hobo knocks on the door and asks if he can do any work around the house in exchange for dinner. Guy says sure, paint that porch out back, and he hands the bum a big brush and a gallon of barn-red house paint. Half an hour later, the hobo is back at the door. "I'm ready for dinner," he says, "and by the way, that ain't a Porsche you got out back, it's a Ferrari."

Frankly, I'd rather fire up the propane heater and listen to it roar like an afterburner, wait for the ice to melt off the wrenches, and lie on my back under the car with the casters of the creeper crunching through a century's accumulation of solidified manure while I try to remember to keep my mouth closed as I wrench away. A friend of mine designed and built an airplane that he flew across both the Atlantic and the Pacific. The only injury it ever caused him was the chipped tooth he suffered when a wrench fell onto his open mouth while he was tightening a hydraulic line under the damn thing. I've never forgotten that.

One thing I did have, besides a porch and a Porsche, was plenty of places to attach a come-along to a beam in the hayloft. A come-along is that aptly named ratcheting, steel-cabled, block-and-tackle device that typically is used to multiply mechanical advantage to make something . . . well, to make something come along. Like a log, or a car in a ditch, or a quarter-ton bathtub that needs to make its way up a stairwell to the second floor. (It's true. I dragged a tub upstairs in the house with the very same come-along, years before.)

So my Porsche engine-dropping technique of necessity started out as a car-lifting exercise. First, after having carefully detached all the necessary connections between engine and car, I put a hydraulic floor jack under the engine/transmission unit, jacked it up just enough to take the load off the engine mounts, and separated the final matings between car and power plant—two simple bolts in the engine compartment and two under the car near the nose of the transmission.

Now the quarter-ton or so of engine and gearbox rested—okay, was perilously balanced—on the saucer-sized pad of my floor jack, plus some wood blocking under each bank of cylinders. With a strong rope attached to the come-along and wrapped through the engine compartment and back up around the rear bumper, I slowly ratcheted the rear end of the car up, away from the engine, while gently pulling the engine/transmission unit just far enough aft to free the transmission shift rod from the shifter coupling at the end of the car's center-console tunnel. And up, and slowly up. The engine came loose, but now I needed to get the car high enough that the engine could be dragged out from beneath it, and this required enough clearance for the high-domed cooling-fan shroud and the mass of the complex fuel-injection manifolding. By the time I had the car high enough, it looked like a cat in heat, ass in the air.

Chancy as all this might sound—and any good Porsche mechanic will wince at the thought of an entire 911 engine being balanced on a Sears floor jack—a 911 engine is in fact relatively easy to remove from the car, particularly with facilities and equipment far better than mine. (Next time, I will use a $150 motorcycle jack, the existence of which I discovered too late. They're four-wheeled, castored floor jacks with a supporting framework broad enough to slip under an entire Harley-Davidson and lift it, free-standing, well off the ground.)

It requires caution and care to ensure that the shifter rod doesn't get bent, that the oil-line connections don't get boogered, that the difficult-to-remove Allen-head screws that hold the axles to the transmission aren't stripped, and that the thin sheet-metal panels that seal the engine into the opening in which it fits aren't misshapen.

A professional Porsche shop can drop a carbureted or simple mechanically fuel-injected 911 engine in forty-five minutes, an hour for a more complex electronically fuel-injected engine like mine, longer for a Turbo.

Yet simply adjusting the valves on a plumbing-encased turbocharged 930 is often accomplished by first dropping the engine for access.

If I had a lovely, warm, flat-floored shop and that motorcycle jack, I'd probably drop the engine routinely. Boy, I could really get into that: "Honey, I'm gonna go out and drop the engine, polish the fan housing, be back in a jiff . . ."

Chapter Seventeen

PORSCHE PEOPLE ARE LIKE MAGPIES

The predominant visual element of a 911 engine, when you peer into the crowded engine compartment, is a bare-metal cooling fan spinning inside a fat-lipped, circular shroud. With the engine running, the whirling blades become a translucent silver disc, but at rest, the assembly looks like the intake of a light helicopter's turbine, with eleven canted compressor blades (some earlier 911s had a less efficient nine) snug inside the annular nozzle.

There was a time, and it was not long ago, when opening an automobile's hood invariably revealed something inarguably mechanical, something recognizably engine-related. "The greasy bits," as the Brits call them. Didn't matter how powerful or expensive the engine, whether it was a big American V8 or a little Japanese four, there was always a shiny sombrero of an air cleaner on top, a fiddly little carburetor on one side, or a Medusa's-nest of ignition wires worming purposefully hither and yon.

"Wow! Lookit all that plumbin'!" was the automotive equivalent of when an aeronautical naïf peeks into an airliner cockpit and exclaims, "Wow! Lookit all them dials!"

But it doesn't happen anymore. Open the hood of just about any new car and you might as well be looking at a dishwasher or clothes dryer.

Engines today are hidden entirely under plastic shrouds, as though the manufacturers are ashamed of their nakedness. (Admittedly, the shrouding does a good job of muffling mechanical noise.) The engine of a twenty-first-century Porsche 911 isn't plasticized, yet peering into its open engine hatch is about like regarding the inspection port of an office-building air-conditioning unit or a limited view of the back side of a small heating plant. And the Porsche Boxster engine can only be seen from *underneath* the car, when it's on a garage lift. All that remains for the owner to see of a Boxster's mechanicals are a bright yellow dipstick and equally colorful oil- and water-fill caps in the trunk.

But that 911 fan . . . it says, "Stand back, we're ready for business." It sucks in a torrent of air and blows it down through the hundreds of cooling fins that surround the six cylinders. Gearheads invariably refer to 911 engines as being air-cooled. This is only partly true. The engines are actually *oil*-cooled, and the air from the fan is supplemental.

Porsche race-engine builder Steve Weiner tells of a client who missed a shift during a race—went from fifth to second instead of fourth—and shredded the fanbelt during the momentary overrev before he dumped the clutch back in. He had taken the precaution of installing a big, red, fan-belt-failure warning light on the dash, but the fact that he was running in second place encouraged him to ignore the light that was yelling YOUR ENGINE IS HISTORY, and he spent the next sixty minutes pushing his 911 as hard as he could—hard enough to eventually finish first, perhaps in part because of the slight added horsepower to the rear wheels that he got as a result of no longer having to drive the fan and alternator. The engine, when disassembled for a post-race teardown, was in perfect shape other than some minor piston-scuffing, thanks to *oil* cooling, since there was no airflow. (The oil admittedly was synthetic Mobil 1, and Weiner doubts that any normal lubricant could have done the same job.)

Obviously, far more BTUs are carried away and dissipated by the constant flow of three gallons of oil through the engine and out to the plump oil tank in the right rear fender and thence to an oil-cooler radiator—or radiators, in the case of high-performance 911s—in the front of the car. So if you want to be really pretentious, correct people by telling them, "No, a 911 is oil-cooled."

There are Porsche sluts who actually say this.

But never mind. I latched onto that aluminum fan and shroud as the object of one of my favorite unskilled car-restoration activities: polishing.

Porsche people are like magpies, attracted to shiny objects—alloy wheels, polished shift knobs, chromed exhaust-pipe outlets—and there are entire magazines and mail-order catalogues devoted to satisfying this lust. There is no part of a Porsche that cannot be "improved" by some aftermarketer, and most of the improvements are—arguably—cosmetic, since we can assume that in most cases, the engineers in Germany know what they are doing far better than does some enthusiastic exhaust-system or torsion-bar modifier in Cupertino or Cleveland.

To tour a Porsche-parts mail-order catalogue is to dive deeply into the psyche of people who view an automobile as the ultimate receptacle for accessorizing. The largest catalogue   *Performance Products,* "the Super Store for your Porsche"—is 240 pages long, and its main competitor, *Tweeks,* trails with 180 pages. Restoration and replacement parts (many made in Mexico) for half-century-old Porsche 356s vie for space with "lifestyle items," which is another name for jackets, caps, sweaters, gloves, key rings, even golf balls that display the Porsche logo or crest.

There is every possible variation on equipment installed at the factory on Porsches. One of the more popular is white instrument dials with black numbers, since stock Porsche dials are black with white numbers. Installation requires that the instruments all be opened and partially disassembled, of course, but apparently, it's worth the effort to some Porsche owners who simply want to be different. When I first visited the Nyack, New York, shop of Rick DeMan, a highly regarded independent Porsche mechanic and racer, he said to me, "I do high-quality mainte-nance and service, and high-performance modifications. I do *not* install white instrument dials."

But am I any different? I wanted my fan to gleam like sterling silver, a dazzling design feature that would cause onlookers to murmur every time I opened the engine hatch. Well, maybe some of them.

So I disassembled the array. The car's alternator, a compact but un-reliable little French unit with a built-in voltage regulator, is inside the fan assembly and is driven by the same belt and pulley that turns the fan. I took the alternator to the local auto-electrics shop to be completely overhauled. Left with the loose fan and the shroud on my workbench, I polished. And polished and polished. Starting with 220-grit and then 600 wet sandpaper, I ground away at the years of neglect, the soft metal pitted by sand and dirt drawn into its whirling vortex.

One of the eleven fanblades was even heavily notched, a good quarter-inch cut, where it had apparently whacked a pebble that somehow got drawn into the engine compartment. Sharp faults of that sort create what are called stress risers, which propagate cracks starting at the tip of the broken vee. On an aluminum airplane propeller, they're considered to be horrendously dangerous and are carefully filed away. If you take out enough metal to turn the sharp little vee into a broad, gentle scallop, the stress riser is eliminated. So I took a Dremel grinder and did the same to my errant fanblade. Probably pointless, since there's vastly less stress on it than there is on a Piper Cherokee prop, but it made me feel as though I was doing something more useful than simply polishing.

Nine-eleven fanblades often get nicked by errant road debris, and sometimes the metal lost as a result is enough to cause concern for the high-revving fan's balance. After all, if you look at the back of a 911's fan, you'll see where small amounts of metal have been drilled out to perfectly balance the unit. The obvious solution is to buy a new fan ($250), but another way to deal with the problem comes via bush pilots who have to deal with broken propellers in the . . . well, in the bush.

Take a metal rod—it can be as simple as a large screwdriver shank—and clamp it horizontally in a vise. Oil the surface of it a bit. Then put the fan on it so that it spins smoothly with the gentle twist of a wrist. When it stops spinning, mark the highest blade with a felt-tip pen. Do this seven times, marking the highest blade each time. (Seven because that is the lowest number of repetitions that will produce a statistically valid result. Why? Don't ask.) If the distribution of the marks is random, for-get it: your fan is balanced close enough for government work. But if the marks are all in one octant of the fan, remove enough metal from the blade 180 degrees opposed to those marks so that the next seven spins produce a random result.

Isn't that wonderfully silly? Think about it and you can easily envision a 911 fan reduced and re-reduced in size in pursuit of balance until it is nothing more than a nubbin with the ghost of eleven former blades vaguely apparent around the hub. But it's the sort of thing that Porsche do-it-themselfers revel in.

Me, I reveled in polishing. Next step was a cloth buffing wheel and jeweler's rouge, and finally a hand polishing with P21S metal-finishing paste. (Simichrompoli, if you can find it, is another good product, a pink German paste favored by the kind of motorcyclists who polish everything including their girlfriends.) The fan and shroud gleamed like the Queen's table silver.

Now what? Aluminum stays polished for about fifteen minutes, then begins to oxidize. There are few mechanical objects as beautiful as an unpainted, polished-aluminum airplane—a Luscombe Silvaire, a rich Texan's P-51, a Howard DGA, a Twin Beech—but anybody who has ever owned one knows that you polish the thing starting at the nose and working toward the tail, and when you reach the tail after about two steady weeks of work, you go back and start polishing at the nose again.

One of my favorite suppliers had become a company called POR-15, which makes an array of enormously tough, epoxy-based primers, paints, coatings, preservatives, and other car restoration supplies. (POR stands for "Paint Over Rust," which you're supposed to be able to do with their flagship product. I once touted POR-15's preservative properties to a far more experienced restorer, however, who looked at me sideways, smiled briefly, and said, "Rust never sleeps." He's probably right.) POR-15 makes a rock-hard coating for aluminum wheels and other highly polished surfaces called Glisten PC, a two-part clear coat that supposedly stands up to hammer blows.

So I carefully coated my fan and shroud with Glisten, let them dry, and stuck them up in the attic with all the other waiting-to-be-reinstalled 911 parts.

Six months later, with the brand-new engine assembled and awaiting its trimmings, I clambered up to the attic to retrieve the fan. Under the impervious coating, a spider web of corrosion had grown everywhere. The once-glistening fan assembly looked like it had spent a month underwater.

Unfortunately, 911 fans and shrouds are pressure-cast aluminum-magnesium alloys, and the quality of the casting depends on a variety of factors. Most are quite porous, and the contamination that builds up in the tiny pores over the years had triggered my corrosion even under the airtight epoxy coating. It's a not-uncommon problem, I discovered from talking to more experienced Porsche restorers.

These pros have tried a variety of approaches to that big, begging-to-be-beautified fan, including powder coating, painting, polishing, anodizing, lacquering, and Kryloning. One problem with applying any coating that adds tangible thickness, however, is that there is already minimal clearance between the fan-blade tips and the inside diameter of the shroud, and anything that decreases that gap can cause problems. Another is that the rotational speed of the fanblades at 6,000 rpm, particularly at the tips, is high enough that even ordinary airborne contaminants will quickly erode even the toughest, shiniest, high-techest coatings. And there's nothing uglier than a once-spectacular gloss red or yellow coating that is gradually being sanded off.

Probably the most logical approach is to gently sandblast the parts until they attain a flat, uniform, grayish, all-business sheen and let it go at that. If you look at a $200,000 Porsche competition engine, that's exactly what the fan looks like.

Me? I disassembled the unit, removed the coating with Aircraft Stripper—the only thing short of a jackhammer that would touch it—and laboriously repolished everything by hand and with the buffing wheel. A coat of pure carnauba wax and . . . well, I'd probably be repolishing everything in a month or two. But as I said, Porsche people are like magpies.

Chapter Eighteen

GIMME A BRAKE

Before I'd put barely 2,000 miles on the back-from-the-dead 911, my muse Steve Weiner perched on my shoulder again and began the whispering thing. He's the guy who'd sold me on the idea of doing $15,000 worth of engine modifications in the first place, by promising me the added power would rip my lips off—an oddly unattractive prospect, though one for which I immediately fell.

"You need better brakes," the Weinermuse whispered. "Turbo brakes."

Better brakes are one of the single simplest yet most expensive modifications that a project-car doofus can add to a 911. From the time the first 911 left the Porsche factory, through the era of the Godzilla 917 race car and then the precedential mid-1970s 911 Turbo, and on to ever-improving Porsche road cars including front-engine, water-cooled 928s and 944 Turbos, the Italian company Brembo has produced for Porsche a series of increasingly powerful disc-brake systems, many of which can be mounted on a variety of older 911s with the help of special brackets, spacers, and sometimes a bit of cutting and grinding.

No car company has ever paid as much engineering attention to brakes as has Porsche. The obvious focus of most sports-car builders has always been speed, acceleration, and handling, a tradition that stretches back to the era of the Alsatian car-builder Ettore Bugatti, who famously said of his fast, enormously successful but primitively braked race cars,

"My cars are made to go, not stop." (And a good thing, too, since Bugattis still had cable-operated mechanical brakes while everybody else had discovered hydraulic brakes operated by vastly more powerful fluid pressure.)

Porsche even to this day is usually at a horsepower disadvantage when compared to its rivals, at least in its production-car-based racers. Today Corvettes, Vipers, Ferraris, Saleens, and Jaguars usually have more pure horsepower than the current-generation 911-based racers can muster, and the disparity was far greater back in the 1950s and 1960s, when Porsches were usually little Davids battling big-engine Goliaths.

But Porsche has always had two things going for it: better brakes, and Teutonic reliability that allowed it to take a licking and come back ticking, as the old John Cameron Swayze Timex commercials had it. (The wonders of truly live television: I to this day remember actually watching the CBS evening newscast during which Swayze strapped a Timex to the screw of an Evinrude suspended in a barrel of water. The outboard wailed for a few seconds, and then Swayze reached down to pull the wristwatch off the prop and demonstrate its survival. It was gone, flung into a thousand pieces. "Well, if we *did* have it, it would still be ticking," the baffled Swayze ad-libbed.)

But I needed better brakes, not a Timex.

The brake job that I did as a result of Steve Weiner's imperative cost me $4,800 just for the parts. (My labor is free, which is about what it's worth.) No, that's not $4,800 for brake pads and turned rotors—your standard "brake job." Even Porsche parts aren't *that* overpriced. What I had waiting in my little cellar workshop after Weiner got through with me was an entire new brake system: huge front and rear four-piston Brembo calipers, massive cross-drilled and vented rotors, a Turbo Porsche master cylinder, Turbo vacuum booster, new brake lines, and high-temp brake fluid—much of it originally designed for the 1,100-horsepower 917 Le Mans and Can-Am car.

The calipers and rotors were specially modified for mounting on my SC by Weiner. The 1989 Turbo rotors that he rehabilitated were originally cast by Porsche with the myriad holes for gas venting and rapid water dissipation that also *look* so cool. (So cool, in fact, that I remember asking a Ferrari PR guy why the full-race 360 Modenas at a Ferrari Challenge race had channeled but solid rotors while the ordinary road 360's rotors were cross-drilled. "Cosmetics," he said.)

"Porsche was one of the first companies to talk about braking in terms of kilowatts and horsepower," says Steve Weiner. "When the 993 Twin Turbo came out in 1996, they touted it as having almost 2,000 hp worth of braking potential." Some say that Porsche got the brakes-equal-horsepower idea from the fact that European heavy trucks use electric "retarders" to help in braking on long downhill runs. "The 3,200-pound 993 Twin Turbo has the same braking capacity as the retarder you'd put on a 42,000-pound Class 7 truck," Weiner points out.

The retarders are basically generators spun by the truck's driveshaft, and when they are energized, they strongly resist the rotation of the driveshaft creating kilowatts of wasted electricity in the process. Retarders are rated in kilowatts to quantify how much braking power the various models offer, and 1.34 kilowatts equal one SAE (U.S.) horsepower.

It's also the way diesel-electric locomotives slow down. Since conventional brake shoes would last only a matter of days under the stress of stopping a freight train as heavy as an entire ship, train drivers (they no longer call them engineers) turn the loco's electric traction motors into generators by reversing the magnetic field, creating enormous drag. The electricity they produce is sent to what's called a dynamic-brake grid— a huge, hairdryer-like nest of wiring at the aft end of the engine's car body—where big fans dissipate the heat into the atmosphere.

There is a difference between European and American horsepower. It's not much, but when I attended the U.S. press introduction of the Ferrari Modena in the summer of 1999, at Meadowlands Racetrack, near New York City, Ferrari had gone to outrageous and expensive effort to collect 400 horses from all over the country—yes, horses, complete with cowboys, handlers, trailers, oats, and hay—in order to collect in the grandstands all of the East Coast press they could attract. This was not hard, since the event was well catered, which is the one thing that is sure to attract journalists.

The point of the exercise was to have a bright-red Modena break from the gate and be followed around the track *very* closely by 400 panting, galloping, hoof-clattering horses, few of whom had even been introduced, much less were friends. Talk about a thundering herd. The idea was that the new Modena's engine had cracked the magical 400-hp barrier.

It had by European DIN [Deutsche Industrie Norm] standards, but by the American SAE [Society of Automotive Engineers] criterion, the result was 395 hp. Spending a zillion dollars to bring 395 nags to New Jersey just didn't have the same ring to it, however.

Brakes such as the set I installed approach the ability to do 1,500 hp worth of work, in a car that probably weighs about 2,500 pounds and on a good day might put out 270 hp. The 2,000-hp Brembos are referred to as "hand-of-God brakes." And they'll absorb 2,000 hp all day long.

Cheap brakes are what separate "pretend" sports cars from automobiles such as Porsches and Ferraris, which can be driven straight from a dealer showroom to an amateur-event racetrack. Try that with a Japanese pretender and its brakes will be steaming and useless after three laps.

Brakes can be equated with horsepower in another sense as well. If a 270-hp race car is going into a corner alongside a lesser-braked 370-hp, it can go deeper into the corner before braking and start its acceleration out the other side sooner. On the right racecourse, that can negate the 100-hp advantage, and out-braking competitors can be more meaningful than their ability to out-accelerate you.

The world's first brakes, appearing immediately after Fred Flintstone invented the wheel, were blocks of wood or metal that bore against a cart's wheel rim and rubbed hard enough to gradually decelerate it. But even in modern times, some brakes have been pretty primitive. I once flew a Russian Antonov An-2 cargo biplane that offered the size and speed of a Winnebago. It had pneumatic brakes, activated by sausage-shaped bladders that inflated to press brake shoes against the inside of a brake drum. I do remember that they wheezed and farted and eventually locked solid while I was trying to taxi back to the ramp, requiring a tractor to come rescue us. The RAF's Spitfires, believe it or not, had a similar system.

Disc brakes were invented by the airplane industry (though certainly not by Antonov) when heavy, fast-moving jets had to be decelerated by brakes on just two wheels, and relatively small ones at that. Airplane brakes face brief but stringent demands. I used to fly a Cessna Citation 500, an economy business jet slow enough that the joke was we'd be rear-ended in flight by Learjets. Nonetheless, I still remember that we were not allowed to take off for thirty minutes after landing on a runway that required major braking effort. Otherwise, if we had to reject the next takeoff, the brakes would still be so hot the tires would catch fire.

Aviation also developed ABS—antilock braking systems. The British company Dunlop made the first, called Maxaret—as in misspelled French for "most stop." The earliest aircraft ABS had electronic sensors that simply detected the instant a wheel stopped turning because it was locked, or sliding, and momentarily released the brake pressure. The process was repeated hundreds of times a minute in a series of slide/roll/slide/roll automatic brake applications, but on a short runway, the pilot could simply hit the brakes as hard as he wished and feel he was probably braking shorter than if he'd modulated or pumped the brakes himself.

It wasn't necessarily true, and to the surprise of many present-day drivers who have been marketed to believe that ABS is perfect, the dirty little secret is that it isn't. Extremely slippery conditions—wet leaves, hydro-plane-inducing water, snow and ice—can fool even the most advanced ABS wheel-speed sensors. Running down our long, steep driveway awhile ago in a Toyota that I was testing for a magazine article, I casually tried a full-ABS panic stop at 30 mph on the carpeting of rain-soaked autumn leaves. The car slid and slid and SLID and slid, the ABS groaning and rattling. I marked the point where we finally stopped, backed up to the top of the hill and tried it again, this time modulating the pedal myself and "threshold braking"—squeezing to the onset of lockup and no more. The Toyota stopped in two-thirds the distance taken by the electronic ABS.

Jaguar brought disc brakes to racing in the early 1950s, on the Le Mans C- and D-Types, at a time when even the Mercedes juggernaut was still relying on huge, finned, inboard drums. (The Jaguar brakes were essentially modified aircraft Maxarets, and the patent for them was held by Dunlop, which refused to sell the brakes to the Huns.) The Jags were slower than the big Ferraris and Benzes, but they'd drive deep past the Italians and Germans at every corner before they had to brake, and they'd be long gone by the time the competition had managed to slow and accelerate again.

What's wrong with drum brakes? As they get hot—which is exactly what brakes are intended to do, to absorb energy—the brake shoes outgas a vapor that, trapped between brake shoe and brake drum, prevents the shoe from firmly contacting the drum to slow it down. Drum brakes have a hard time dissipating that heat, since the drum itself, shaped like a large frying pan, encloses all of the heat-creating parts. Disc brakes are open-air mechanisms.

The drums also expand, increasing the distance between drum and brake shoe. Brake hard once and it doesn't matter, for everything will have cooled down before the next stoplight. Brake hard for three or four race-track corners, however, and the next one will find you with the pedal on the floor and the brake shoe still reaching for the expanded drum. That's called brake fade.

Nor did it do race cars much good when changing drum-brake shoes during a pit stop was a time-consuming process roughly akin to what the Chevy dealer would have spent an hour doing with your '69 Impala up on the lift. Disc-brake pads can be exchanged in seconds.

Any pro race-car driver will tell you that the most productive expenditures you can make as an amateur racer are to first take a competition-driving course and learn to drive. Second, buy better brakes. And only when you've done that, spend what's left on making the engine stronger.

"Americans who want high-performance cars have no qualms about spending $10,000 to making a car accelerate faster," Steve Weiner says, "but they recoil in horror if you suggest they spend half that amount to stop the car faster. In Europe, it's the opposite. They'll spend money on braking and handling, and uprating the engine comes last. Adding horsepower before paying any attention to the brakes is all part of our culture."

Ask almost any enthusiast driver which is the hardest pedal to use and they'll probably say, "The gas and brake are no-brainers—you just push 'em—so it has to be the clutch." Wrong. Few of us, and I'm not a member of the elite group, have the experience and talent to brake correctly. In a panic situation, we either brake too gently or, if the accident is truly imminent, so hard we lock up the wheels. Which is why the Germans (Bosch, specifically) perfected the British ABS concept and then added "brake-assist" electronics to apply extra braking when the microchip senses a too-puny panic stop.

"You can teach somebody in a day or two how to read a corner, how to go around it, how to pick an apex and immediately look ahead to the corner coming up, but learning to decelerate a car at its maximum is a feel, a matter of experience, and many people never develop that feel," Weiner says. "It's the toughest thing to teach a driver."

My new Brembos and I, we look forward to learning.

Chapter Nineteen

AMBULANCE GUY

very Thursday and Friday morning, the alarm goes off a few minutes before six, and I put on my uniform. A blue shirt with "EMS" in big white letters on the back; heavy dark-blue trousers that cops call tactical pants, with cargo pockets, radio holders, and a variety of snaps and buckles; and black quasimilitary boots. I'm a volunteer ambulance driver, and there are times I wish I had Brembos on the top-heavy, ill-handling rigs I have to drive.

Actually, all I put on is the shirt plus my socks and skivvies, because then I climb back into bed with my pager next to me. Once a month or so, it'll go off when I've fallen back asleep—a frantic BEEPBEEPBEEP-BEEP and then a siren sound, followed by "Covac, respond to 51 Reservoir Road . . ." But usually, I'm safe till I get up for good at 7:30 or so.

I'm on duty from six in the morning until six in the evening those two days. Some days, the pager won't make a sound. Others, it'll go off three or four times, occasionally when we're already off on a call, which means the dispatcher will need to try and summon a second ambulance crew. We're all volunteers, and sometimes it's hard to find anybody else available. When that happens, we call the duty crew from the next town to the north. They know they can depend on us to do the same for them.

Still, our small Hudson Valley town is pretty well equipped: two fully stocked modular ambulances, each with a big rolling-ER box behind the cab; a third compact, van-size ambulance with four-wheel drive, for winter emergencies in our hilly area; and what's called a fly car. They're all garaged in our own big, modern, four-bay building complete with a lounge, bunks, cable television, broadband Internet access, and a big Hitachi projection TV that seems to know only one hue—purple.

The fly car is a lights-and-sirens-bedecked SUV that is usually driving around in the hands of whoever the duty crew chief is. He or she is an EMT who can go straight to the scene of an emergency—the "first responder"—while the ambulance comes separately.

I hate those calls. "Driver 41, go direct . . ." Because even after living here for thirty-two years, my mind sometimes goes blank when I hear the address to which I'm supposed to speed. Orrs Mills Road . . . where the hell is Orrs Mills Road? Penny Lane? Never heard of it. I once went twice completely around the traffic circle in the middle of town unable to remember which exit was Angola Road, the flashing strobes and wailing sirens ensuring that everyone knew this was one confused ambulance. We carry a route book filled with specific directions to every street, road, and lane in town, but sometimes, with the radio babbling and a medic in back yelling directions, even those become a blur.

The worst thing you can say to a paramedic or even a simple emergency medical technician is "Oh, so you're an ambulance driver!"

"I am NOT an ambulance driver," they will tell you, for the driver is *way* down the EMS food chain. I *am* a driver, for my frequent travels on writing assignment don't allow me the long, unbroken stretch during which to attend the four-month, four-evenings-a-week course for certification as a basic EMT. So driving is all I can contribute to Covac— the Cornwall Volunteer Ambulance Corps.

It's a strangely confrontational affair, this EMS business, and few civilians have any idea how constant and touchy the battle of emergency services providers is. EMTs versus ER doctors. Doctors versus nurses. Professional paramedics versus volunteer EMTs. Fire-department EMTs versus ambulance EMTs. Nurses versus everybody. Everybody versus the dispatchers. At motor-vehicle accident scenes, the cops hate the state troopers and the staties think the local cops are amateurs. Fire companies are rivalrous and ambulance corps criticize each others' rigs.

Criticism is constant, though usually unspoken. This EMT is way too excitable, that one doesn't know what she's doing. The ER doc is a jerk just out of med school, the nurse is a pain in the ass because she's all over you for bringing in a frequent flyer who didn't need to come to the ER in the first place. (Frequent flyers are the all-too-common malcontents who call the ambulance as a kind of lie-down taxicab. Even our bucolic little town has a rooming house full of welfare recipients who call us whenever they're bored, drunk, psychotic, or simply need a ride.)

It's not surprising that ambulance-call incidents are often noted in the duty log in "versus" shorthand: "Time 1832, location Shore Road, man versus chain saw." "Time 0650, location Salisbury Mills RR station, man versus train." EMS is not an affair of cooperating equals but of a hierarchy of elements defined by money, repute, badges, and other markers of status.

I suspect that in their training, EMTs and particularly paramedics are instilled with the notion that they are actually front-line doctors—maybe even more than that, since they work not in brightly lit, well-equipped operating rooms but on vomit-slick bathroom floors, urine-steeped bedrooms, dark stairwells, and cold roadsides. We volunteers don't make a dime, of course, but even the professional EMT or para has about the lowest ratio of salary to responsibility of any job I can think of. A basic EMT makes about $25,000 a year. Maybe twice that, tops, for a paramedic at the top of the ladder. And that's for sixty-hour weeks with twelve-hour shifts.

As a volunteer, I'm a rarity, an outlander. White-collar guys, professional women, execs, upper-middle-class people with comfortable jobs like mine don't volunteer to be firefighters or EMS people. They can afford to make donations, contributions, pay cash. For them, the long nights in the ambulance-bays bunk room watching whatever WWF match the crew chief has chosen on the cable TV can't compete with the comforts of home. Our people hang out at the bays because probably they don't *have* cable TV wherever they live, and they rarely have a PC and broadband Internet access.

Covac is made up of a couple of schoolteachers, two insurance agents, a nurse, a lab technician, several professional EMTs and a paramedic who volunteer their off-duty time, retirees, some high schoolers who'd rather do this than go out for football, an Air Force Reserve sergeant, a New York City fireman, and the local appliance repairman. I'm the only one who gets to say, "I have to go to Johannesburg on an assignment next week," and when I go to the City for a meeting, it's assumed I mean Newburgh, not Manhattan.

What particularly amuses the hard-bitten crews, however, is wondering what I'll be driving when I show up at the bays in response to an alarm. The others pull up in their Corollas and Neons and pickups, green emergency light twirling on the dashboard, and I'll arrive in a Bentley Arnage, a Lamborghini Murcielago, the latest Lexus, a prototype Chevy convertible pickup truck—whatever test car I have in the driveway that week.

Sometimes, I even take the yellow Porsche.

Whatever my duty car is, I ready it the night before, making sure it's parked pointing down the driveway, to spare the seconds I'd have to spend turning around. My driving glasses, an ambulance-corps ball cap, and a two-way Motorola are ready on the passenger seat. The green emergency light is plugged in and on the glareshield, and the key is in the ignition.

When my pager does go off, I'm a little like a pilot who hears the scramble klaxon, running for my F-16, strapping in as I taxi, getting the cockpit organized and making radio calls on the roll as I head like Tom Cruise toward the dogfight.

That's silly, of course. One of the most dangerous things in medical care of any sort is haste, and I'm supposed to get myself to the ambulance bays in the same careful manner I'd drive to the post office. (It's also official procedure never to run, always walk, at the scene of an emergency call. It frightens onlookers and victims' relatives and is risky in any case.)

Yet they keep track of our "response time" and boast that Covac averages four minutes from the time the dispatcher sends the emergency call to the moment the ambulance is rolling and the driver radios underway. It's one reason we have been officially adjudged to be the best ambulance unit in the entire county. But for me to make it from house to the bays in four minutes requires a heavy throttle foot.

One day, driving the yellow 911 to the bays in response to a medical-emergency page, I saw a state trooper in a familiar speed-trap spot and slowed from 75 to 65. "I have my headlights on, all four hazard flashers blinking, and the green emergency strobe going. He knows what's go-ing on," I thought as I slowed.

Still, he chased me. Troopers are like dogs that smell a tire. He didn't catch me until I pulled into my emergency-crews-only parking slot and yelled as I dashed for the ambulance, "You're not supposed to speed! What kind of call you got?"

"Cardiac arrest," I yelled as I piled into the rig. ("I'll see your siren and raise you twelve strobes plus an air horn that would blow the Super Chief off the tracks.") Even a cop knows that a stopped heart doesn't wait for a traffic ticket.

What the cop didn't know was that our call was in fact for an old woman who'd probably sat on her MedicAlert button.

Ambulances are ill-handling pigs, so I need to take a deep breath and transition from the 911 or loaner Lamborghini to one of our big dualie, mod-box Fords. Ambulances are built on relatively unsophisticated truck chassis, and it doesn't help that "the box" needs to be pretty high, so a stretcher can be loaded at a level about three feet off the ground. The compartment is well-built of lightweight aluminum, but there's a lot of heavy stuff back there—cabinetry, medical equipment, wiring, oxygen tanks, and the like—and the rig's center of gravity is pretty perilous.

I'm our corps' "driving instructor." All it means is that I give a lecture, show an excruciatingly boring National Safety Council videotape, and present our drivers with a written quiz every six months or so. Most of the talking involves trying to get them to slow down, since the sound of a siren adds 10 or 20 mph to anybody's throttle foot, and an ambulance doing 70 or 80 is far more dangerous than whatever emergency it's traveling toward.

Hollywood always shows an ambulance wailing toward the hospital in a torrent of sirens and strobes. They have it backward. We travel *to* emergencies with lights and noise, but once there's a patient aboard, the ride turns smooth, gentle, and quiet no matter how bad the injuries are. (The one exception is a cardiac arrest.) Because with somebody on the stretcher, even if they're dying, there will typically be an EMT and a paramedic back there, unbelted and moving around, starting IVs and talking on the radio to the hospital, and the last thing they need is to be doing it locked inside a speeding truck. And you don't know how bad a pothole feels until you've hit it hard with somebody with a broken pelvis lying on the stretcher screaming at you.

Even when the situation is so bad that a medevac helicopter has been called in, calm reigns. When a motorcyclist used a guardrail as a human bread knife and totally severed both arms and most of one leg—he'd been clocked at 115 mph in a 30 and cops from two towns away were chasing him—the helo landed on the soccer field of a local prep school. Our EMTs loaded his arms onto the stretcher, still in their leathers, and we drove him to the LZ. I was stunned to see how unhurriedly, methodically, and competently the flight paramedics worked on the poor kid before even unloading him from the ambulance. (He died nonetheless, once in flight and, after being briefly revived, once more at the trauma center.)

When people learn that I'm an EMS volunteer, they often say, "Oh, that must be *so* rewarding, helping people that way." No. It's fun is what it is. Yes, there's a certain amount of satisfaction, particularly on the rare occasions when patients or their relatives actually bother to thank you rather than bitch that you should have arrived sooner, but for the most part, the excitement and adrenaline are the major reward.

Which is why some people who do EMS work for a living come home and continue doing it for free as volunteers. Some of them are accident junkies. A UCLA folklore professor, Timothy Tangherlini, has even written a fascinating book, *Talking Trauma: Paramedics and Their Stories,* about the manner in which EMS people compete to tell the most gruesome tales from their experience (and, sometimes, their imagination) to establish their rank and bragging rights.

Even in our little EMS corps, a "good call" is not what you might expect—one that finds a false alarm, say, or a little old lady who fell but now is fine. Not long ago, one of our EMTs griped at the corps' monthly meeting that a few members were "jumping calls"—responding to week-end alarms and tearing off with the ambulance when they weren't even on duty. "I get a Sunday-afternoon call for rectal bleeding," she griped, "and I'm all alone. But if a *good* call gets toned out, like an MVA roll-over on the Thruway, you got EMTs comin' out of the woodwork." (MVA is copspeak for motor-vehicle accident.)

That's a good call.

I'd been on the job only two months when, inevitably, I got my first bloody, gruesome one.

"Don't worry about it," a friend in the corps had told me. "It's going to happen, it's going to be awful, but at the time, it won't bother you. Maybe it will later."

It was an accident on the New York State Thruway, and I most vividly remember our rubber-gloved EMT carefully picking up a small piece of the driver's brain and putting it in the car next to her, as though it was necessary to make sure that all the parts were accounted for. The side of her head was gone. Her husband and their young son, still alive, were medevaced out by a helicopter that landed in the broad, grassy median of the highway while summer tourist traffic gaped. When it's this bad, you have to erect big blue tarps around the wreck or they'd simply park and stare.

The woman had rolled and literally looped her SUV on a long, downhill straightaway of the New York State Thruway. She'd apparent-ly gotten her left-side tires onto the rumble strip—the corrugated con-crete on the shoulder that's intended to wake up drowsy drivers who begin to drift off the road—and had jerked the steering wheel to the right in surprise. Maybe she *had* gone to sleep for a moment and awoke with a start.

That started the rear end of the Ford Explorer swinging to the left, and she corrected way too forcefully and counterskidded hard to the right. When a tall car like an SUV with a high center of gravity slides sideways, just about anything can trip it and send it into a roll, even just the grip of the tires sliding or the impact of a crack between two slabs of concrete. Her car's cargo area was loaded to the roofline with what looked like office supplies, putting its CG even higher.

I rolled an SUV once—a Jeep Liberty—and it happened so fast that the truck went through 450 degrees of roll at only about 20 mph, ending up on its right side, before I even knew what had happened. My injuries, since I was fully belted in and the impact was sideways and therefore the airbags didn't deploy, were limited to my glasses falling off and a ticket for "reckless driving." Which wasn't the case but was the opinion of a sheriff who arrived twenty minutes later. Nobody had witnessed the accident, though it cost me $1,000 to hire a local lawyer to quash the charge. (In Virginia, where it happened, a reckless-driving charge is as bad as a DUI, and it can't be ignored.)

My Jeep crash took place at the press introduction of the brand-new Liberty, near Charlottesville. I was off by myself, on a back road, driving one of the test-fleet cars that I hadn't had a chance to drive earlier that day. The crushed car was quickly put onto a flatbed under a tarp and hauled away. None of the other journalists present was told about the accident, and I was asked to keep my mouth shut, which I meekly did. Stupid of me, since the other journalists had a right to know that the car's handling was subpar, but I was dreadfully embarrassed to have wrecked a press car for the first time in my career.

A month or so later, *Autoweek* magazine rolled a Liberty on a test track while putting it through its paces, and published the news while questioning the new car's stability. DaimlerChrysler professed shock and surprise. "Nobody has ever rolled a Liberty before," they fibbed.

Soon thereafter, the Liberty was slightly modified, before customer deliveries began, to lower its CG an inch or so.

My next fatality call came that fall, Thanksgiving weekend, also on the thruway. An elderly couple from Massachusetts had apparently driven past the exit they wanted, a few miles back. Rather than go to the next exit and reverse course, the husband for some unaccountable reason—other than the fact that he was in his eighties—decided to make a U-turn through a break in the median divider, spang across two lanes of heavy holiday traffic in the middle of the afternoon.

A thirty-ton tanker hit the Chrysler Concorde sedan square amidships after laying down 200 feet of black rubber in a desperate attempt to stop from what was probably a routine 70 mph. As I ran with a trauma bag toward the scene—it's okay to run when you're facing carnage—a trooper laughed and said, "Take your time, they ain't goin' nowhere." I caught up to our local fire chief, in full turnout gear. "I got a deer in the trunk of my car that isn't as dead as those two," he said.

The couple were essentially compacted—almost bloodless and almost charming, the man with his lifeless hand atop his wife's lap, though the white bone of his forearm poking through the wrist was a jarring note. One tiny trickle of blood from the woman's ear inched its way down her parchment skin.

Wherever EMS crews are, they have their own special challenges, whether it's tractor rollovers in Iowa, hypothermia in Minnesota winters, or house-to-house combat in East LA. Ours are the six-mile stretch of New York State Thruway that runs through our turf, and, of all things, mountains.

The Hudson Highlands aren't mountains by Colorado standards, but they're steep and accessible enough—sixty miles north of Manhattan and laced with hiking trails—that a lot of hikers get into a lot of trouble. In the last couple of years, we've had one rockslide death, a number of hikers who have fallen off cliffs and somehow survived, and bee stings.

Yes, bee stings. Anaphylactic shock can kill you. A neighbor of mine died on a yacht miles off the Maine coast some years ago when he got stung and didn't have his Albuterol injector. Who knew a bee would do a Lindbergh that far out over the Atlantic?

Our last bee-sting-shock case was a middle-aged hiker from Manhattan whose companion happened to be an MD, a psychiatrist. She was frightened enough by his labored breathing and swelling extremities to put out a 911 call on her cell phone. A powerful young fireman and I were the first to the trailhead, and Eric and I alternately humped a duffel full of medical gear and an oxygen tank a mile up a steep trail to finally find the couple, by this time with the help of a State Police helicopter that had joined the hunt.

Twenty minutes behind us were more EMTs and firefighters, with a heavy metal-framed stretcher so we could carry the guy out. "Please," he said with a sarcastic eye-roll as they arrived, sweating under rescue gear and emergency backpacks, "half-sick, I'm more capable than you people are healthy. I hike all the time. I'll walk out, boys, and you can follow me."

Where are the bees when you really need them?

Chapter Twenty

PORSCHE IMPERFECT

I f anybody tells you the engineers at Porsche are automotive geniuses, ask them why those geniuses couldn't, even in the 1980s, design an automotive air-conditioning system that worked. In a time when the a/c in any American economy car could make ice, 911s were famous for lugging around a heavy, primitive system that gently breathed wisps of barely unwarm air. And the required apparatus added enormously to the clutter in the increasingly tight engine compartment.

One problem that confronted Porsche's engineers was that they lived in Stuttgart, not Houston, Phoenix, or Palm Springs. Their idea of hot-weather testing in those days was a weekend on the Riviera. Geographic—and societal—distance from a major market had a lot to do with why Jaguars used to overheat in traffic, why Chevy couldn't sell Novas in South America (*no va* means no go in Spanish), and why the first Toyotas exported to the U.S. couldn't deal with cold weather.

When Toyota execs in the early '60s began to hear reports that its cars wouldn't start in northeast winters, they were baffled. Parts of Japan experience severely cold winters, and Japanese Toyota owners had never complained of start-up difficulties. Toyota sent managers to live in New Jersey to observe this strange car culture at close range, and they discovered to their horror that during the winter, Americans sometimes parked their cars in an unheated garage or even left it in the driveway or at the curb, forgodsakes. A Japanese Toyota owner would never have left such a valuable artifact out in the cold but would have swaddled, blanketed, and warmed it, perhaps even somehow brought it into the house, so of *course* Toyotas never had problems with cold weather in Japan.

Porsche's engineers were also hindered by the fact that the source of energy for the system—the compressor and the main condenser—sat at the absolute opposite end of the car from the cooling breezes that meet a moving 911's nose. So the bulky, belt-driven compressor was hung from the engine on a bracket that required the compressor to be removed any time even the slightest engine work was required. And the main condenser radiator was mounted directly above the hot engine, between it and its source of cooling air, under the grille on the engine-compartment lid.

More was needed, so Porsche mounted a second condenser under the nose of the car. This required fifteen feet of leak-prone rubber plumbing running under the belly of the beast from the compressor to the front condenser, via a dessicator in the left front wheelwell, and back again. Plus a fancy electric fan in the trunk of the car that blew cooling air down through the condenser. Oh, and that frequently caught fire in certain 911 models, occasionally burning the car to a crisp.

Remind me again why Porsche engineers are geniuses?

Okay, let's be fair. Porsche is a tiny company, in automotive-universe terms, with limited resources. Little did they know, when they introduced the 911 in 1963, that they would still be selling the same basic car thirty-five years later. Indeed, there were several attempts to kill the damn thing and concentrate on building either a proper front-engine/rear-drive V8 grand touring car or a sporty four-door with wider appeal. But Porsche was stuck, thanks in part to the 911's enormous racing success in Turbo guise and in part to the car's ascension to icon status. Literally. Two global brands I can think of that have patented a shape are Coca-Cola of its pinch-waisted bottle and Porsche of its two-teardrops profile.

When 911 mavens have nothing better to do, they sit around listing the design failings of their favorite car, and the list is surprisingly long.

Besides the cumbersome and ineffective air-conditioning, 911s are notorious for a variety of inexplicable—or at least not explicable by me—
faults.

Most 911s have an oil cooler in the right front fenderwell, and it's
fed by two large, soft-brass pipes that run externally along the belly, under the passenger-door sill. They are critical conduits, of course—"the
car's aorta," as one 911 owner described them—yet are located exactly
so that some unknowing mechanic's floor jack is sure to crush them.

The flow of oil through those pipes is controlled by a big aluminum-
housing thermostat unit in the right rear wheelwell. Between the spray
of road rubbish that constantly splashes it and the fact that the threads
for the heavily torqued compression fittings on the thermostat are also
dead-soft aluminum, it is impossible to put a wrench to any of those four
joints without stripping the threads.

The 911's oil tank has a dipstick, but if the car has been parked with
its engine off for several days, the dipstick will be dry. You might be half
a quart low or your sump plug might have been knocked off and drained
the tank. The dipstick will tell you nothing. It's also mounted in a way
that makes it easy to drop it all the way into the tank. (Many a 911 is driving around with two or three dipsticks rattling around in the bottom of
the oil tank, since it's easier to buy a new one than it is to fish out the
offender.)

So how do you tell how much oil is in your 911? Well, there's a nice
little oil level gauge right on the dashboard. Except that if the engine
is running at anything above idle, the gauge will be in the red, shouting
that you are out of oil. It is only accurate with the oil warmed to running
temperature, the car sitting dead level, and the engine at idle for at least
a minute. Between the semi-useless dipstick and the special-circumstances
oil-level gauge, the 911 is the only production car I know of that en-
genders endless discussions among its owners as to how much oil to add
during an oil change.

Nine-elevens like mine came from the factory with rather basic,
primitive fuel-injection systems called CIS (Constant-Injection System),
which supplies lots of fuel all the time at relatively high pressure, with

the unused excess routed back to the gas tank. They are warily famed for their exploding airboxes. If the engine backfires during startup, which happens if sudden climatic and temperature changes confuse the CIS system's archaic microprocessor, the small but potent gasoline explosion inside the induction system blows apart the expensive plastic airbox. Porsche never fixed the problem, but the aftermarket industry quickly came up with a cheap pop-off valve, much like a toilet-tank flapper valve, that could be epoxied in place by do-it-yourselfers.

Some other Porsche paradoxes? The list is long:

- It's difficult to jack a 911 safely for do-it-yourself maintenance with a standard garage floor jack, for there are no reinforced jacking points on the floorpan, which deforms easily. You either put a special floor-jack adapter into the car's two external jacking points—where the emergency tire-changing jack fits—or put the car on a service-station lift.

- A 911's heating system, which is ineffective at best, is a VW Bug holdover. It consists of muffs welded around the exhaust pipes on each side of the car. Ambient air is blown through them to be warmed by the hot pipes, and the heated—barely—air then travels into the cabin. But if there's a leak in those pipes, the heating system very efficiently pumps carbon monoxide into the cabin as well.

- Unless you're rich enough to afford both a Porsche and twin toddlers, a 911's two minuscule backseats are both useless and ugly, good for nothing but grocery bags. Worse, they fill the space where the 911's engine should have gone: *ahead* of the rear axle, just as it does in the thoroughly modern, backseatless Boxster.

- The 911's inside door handles are thin, plastic, and notorious for snapping off. Apologists say it's not a design flaw but a design feature, so you can't "overstress" the rest of the door-opening mechanism. What a good idea—so much easier than making a suitably strong door mechanism, ja?

- Targa tops leak, virtually without exception. Their owners deserve it.
- The low-oil-pressure warning light doubles as the hand brake–on warning light on some 911 models. If one of these 911s is parked with the hand brake pulled and the engine running, there's no idiot-light warning that oil pressure has suddenly failed. Porsche's excuse is that this provides a frequent check that the bulb hasn't failed. But there are other ways to accomplish this—like having a separate oil-pressure light come on before every engine start.
- A 911's climate-control levers and knobs are a primitive set of multiple sliders working through wire-wrapped cables just like those that operate your Toro lawnmower's throttle. (Remember, we're talking here about an expensive luxury sports car.) There are three on the dashboard and two more down between the front seats, and simply getting defogging air to the windshield requires operating four separate controls. Some 911 owners haven't to this day figured out how their heating/cooling systems work.

Mine would operate relatively simply, since I decided to eighty-six the entire air-conditioning system and strip the car of its heavy compressor and network of hoses. Unfortunately, I made this decision *after* spending $900 to buy an entire, brand new a/c system, in a rash of buy-this, buy-that, ohmygod-lookit-what-else-you-can-get enthusiasm engendered by my first naïve look into the universe of Porsche-parts mail-order catalogues.

Anybody want to buy a complete, unused, brand-new a/c system for a 911SC?

Chapter Twenty-One

GEARBOX

The first real evidence I got that my Porsche had gone through a few hard knocks came to light when I opened up its transmission. Nothing as obvious as chipped-off gear teeth that came out with the drained oil, but there were major signs that the gearbox had taken some hits. A bent mainshaft, for one thing, and some terminally worn bushings, for another.

Wondering what your car has been through is like thinking about how your wife lost her virginity. On the one hand you don't want to know, on the other you can't help daydreaming the worst. Hard to imagine how somebody could mistreat a gearbox that badly, though. A lifetime of terrible shifting? Sliding it into a curb sideways at speed? Driving it down a flight of marble steps for a movie?

I've never in my life been inside a transmission. They're a mystery to me and for the most part still are. A Porsche 911SC's transmission is a remarkably compact, light, and simple device. The transmission itself (not counting the clutch bell housing and the differential) is about the size and shape of half a rural mailbox—a tiny thing, really. Maybe it's a little too tiny, for the Type 915 gearbox, as it's officially called, suffers its share of shifting faults, balky synchromeshes, and outright failures.

In an attempt to forestall such problems, serious Porscheniks spend hours, days, *weeks* discussing the merits of various expensive, highly specialized natural and synthetic transmission lubricants. Oddly enough, the rest of the world is happy to let cars live out their entire lives without a thought for what kind of oil is in their transmissions. And if your manual-transmission Toyota needs a top-up, the dealer puts in some "gear lube" and that's it.

Because of its location directly between the rear wheels, a 911's gearbox is in fact a transaxle: a transmission-plus-differential unit from which the drive axles sprout like arms from the shoulders of a little aluminum R2D2. A conventional transmission transmits its power to a longitudinal driveshaft, typically issuing from the aft end of the gearbox. A transaxle drives lateral axles directly. Ferdinand Porsche invented the transaxle, and the Porsche transaxles installed in his enormous 1930s Auto Union (today called Audi) grand prix cars look almost exactly like 911 gearboxes.

An old-fashioned front-engine/rear-wheel-drive car has its engine and transmission up front, bolted firmly together, with a long driveshaft leading to a differential about the size of a bowling ball at the back of the car. The differential turns the driveshaft's rotation 90 degrees left and right and thus directly to the rear wheels. (It also allows those wheels to turn at slightly different speeds, which they must do when going around a corner, since the outside wheel is traveling farther than the inside wheel. Which is why they're called differentials.)

This arrangement leaves the bulk of the drivetrain—the engine and transmission—sitting way up in the front of the car, creating an unfortunate forward weight bias. So if you're building a car like a Ferrari Maranello, a modern Corvette, or certain BMWs, you go to the added expense of using a transaxle. The engine stays up front, but the gearbox migrates to the rear of the car and is combined with the differential, thus somewhat evening out the balance of the heaviest pieces of the drivetrain.

Perhaps what this means is that Porsche 911s actually should have had front-wheel drive, with the engine in back and the transaxle up front. Never mind.

A 911 transaxle unbolts easily from the engine and can actually be physically picked up and plopped onto a workbench. Even by a writer.

Once you've got it up there, it comes apart pretty easily. At least it does if you have the factory shop manual.

There are several how-to-work-on-a-911 books on the market, but with the exception of the two excellent albeit expensive volumes published by Bentley and covering the SC (1978–83) and the Carrera (1984–89), the rest are abbreviated, fuzzily illustrated, cheaply done books that will lead you through a variety of minor repairs but that shouldn't be relied upon for the big jobs. Jobs like getting inside a 911's engine or transmission.

For that, you need the factory shop manual. It is cumbersome and hideously expensive. A new 911SC factory manual typically costs about $600, depending on where you buy it, although used volumes show up frequently on eBay.

The reason it is cumbersome devolves from the fact that unlike most cars, the 911 was always a work in progress. It was a car that stayed in production from 1964 through 1998 in six basic iterations and with detail changes and improvements on a yearly, sometimes monthly basis. So the manual for a 911SC consists of a set of three, fat, loose-leaf books dealing with the basic made-in-1964 911, plus four smaller supplements encompassing the changes and differences. The newer your 911 is, the more supplement volumes you have to buy.

It's also a fact of Porsche life that the manuals never get corrected or reissued in new editions. If there are mistakes in the manual—and there are—they get fixed in "technical service bulletins," which also must be bought and consulted to do the job right.

Still, you need the factory manual if you're going to do any serious work on your 911, like taking apart the transmission. Be aware, however, that it's not a how-to book for the DIYer. It is intended for people who are already professional mechanics and who have also attended a Porsche technician training course and been taught in a classroom the basic skills of a 911 mechanic. The factory manual will detail the sequence of procedures and has 1970s-quality photos to make the complex steps slightly clearer, but it assumes you know how to "drive seal into seat" or "secure flange nut by notching." *What* to do is clearly specified. *How* to do it often is not.

I disassembled my transmission to the point where I had a variety of small parts, an empty transmission housing, some loose gears, and two large, complex clusters of very expensive-looking gears and synchromesh mechanisms on their shafts. I didn't touch the differential other than to unbolt the transmission from it. Which could have meant that when I finally drove my repainted, re-engined, re-interioried, re-everythinged 911SC for the first time, I would find that the ring-and-pinion set had gone tits-up and should have been replaced when I had everything apart. That would at least give me the opportunity to choose and install a new quick-acceleration rear-end ratio, right?

Now I needed an expert, to deal with the crucial heart of the transmission. The name that usually comes to mind when U.S. Porsche people discuss gearbox mavens is Gary Fairbanks. Fortunately, Fairbanks's shop is in Norwalk, Connecticut, about an hour's drive from my New York house.

"Jeez, Fairbanks, he's a crotchety guy," one Porsche owner told me. "He hung up on me when I asked him what gear ratios to pick," another said. "Told me he'd install the gears, but picking them wasn't his job." I telephoned Fairbanks with foreboding, fully expecting to be told that if I wanted to make believe I was a mechanic, I could make believe I'd do the whole job.

"Hmmm . . . that's interesting," Fairbanks said when I proposed to bring him the two mainshafts with their gear clusters plus the ancillary pieces to assess and rejuvenate. "Nobody's ever done it that way before, but it makes sense. You'll save some money if I don't have to do the whole job. Of course, I can't give you my usual guarantee, because you'll be reassembling everything yourself and I have no idea how competent you are, but yeah, bring the stuff over and let me take a look at it."

When I arrived, Fairbanks immediately saw that my transmission housing was junk, its bushing seats too worn to do further duty. He also quickly stripped the input mainshaft of its gears and determined that it was badly bent—nothing discernible to the eye, of course, but rolling it across a dead-flat, milled surface revealed the disparity. It went thunk-thunk-thunk instead of rrrrrrr, if you get my drift. He patted me on the back and sent me home, told me he'd put everything right.

Two days later, my gears were ready. Fairbanks, who has gotten a reputation for being overbearing and demanding among Porsche owners who, I suspect, are themselves *truly* overbearing and demanding, offered to save me a good part of the drive back to Norwalk by meeting me halfway. (It was on his route home but a kindness I'd never expected.)

Fairbanks had straightened and saved the enormously expensive input shaft by giving it a few smart whacks with a bronze-headed mallet—one that he'd bought specifically to do my job—and the shaft now trued out perfectly. "That's the most bent one I've ever straightened," he admitted. The synchros were all rebuilt, the gears checked, and Fairbanks had found in his used-parts pile a good 915 case to replace my ruined one. He provided me with a gasket set for reassembly of the transaxle, a one-job quantity of sealant, and a few words of immeasurably good advice. We shook hands and parted company in a motel parking lot near the Tappan Zee Bridge.

Chapter Twenty-Two

CAR AND DRIVER DAYS

I parted company with the world of suits and salaried jobs on far less friendly terms.

The end began in the fall of 1974, when I became the editor of *Car and Driver,* the country's most imaginative and influential auto-enthusiast magazine. At the moment, I thought it was the culmination of my career as a magazine journeyman.

I once heard my *über*boss, Bill Ziff, the billionaire owner of the Ziff-Davis Publishing Company, say in a speech that, "To be the editor of a Ziff-Davis magazine is a calling." At the time, I heard it as "appalling." Which was far closer to the truth in my case, for the brief year and a half that I spent being battered by my staff, my bosses, and my advertisers.

"Congratulations," said a Ziff-Davis senior vice-president who stuck out his hand when it was announced that I had been anointed. "Now you're a member of management." Oh dear, I thought, nobody told me *that.*

Through a series of imaginative editors-in-chief, *Car and Driver* had grown from just another sports-car magazine into a snarky, intelligent, iconoclastic monthly that was never afraid to pan a bad car, never afraid to do outrageous things, never shrank from calling the shots as it saw them. Management saw it differently, since all of Ziff-Davis's special-interest magazines were strongly advertising-driven. Insulting the people who bought the ad space was, as far as the suits were concerned, the worst thing an editor could do.

One of the most notorious photos that ever ran in *C/D* was a road-test lead-off illustration that had been given the go-ahead by a delightfully arrogant and acerbic editor-in-chief, a predecessor of mine named Leon Mandel. "The Opel in the Junkyard" was typical of the constant editorial/advertising battle. *C/D* had decided that the Opel of that era, newly imported into the U.S. by General Motors, was a piece of junk, and it didn't want to leave any room for doubt. It shot the car against a background of rusty, cruddy, crumpled beaters in a Long Island auto-salvage yard. GM was not amused and pulled all its advertising for six months.

The man who had initially turned *C/D* away from the veddy tweedy, Jegyewars-are-splendid-motorcars approach of *Road & Track* (our main competition) was a former ad copywriter, David E. Davis Jr. Davis is universally acknowledged as the editor who, with the enthusiastic connivance of burly, trash-talking contributor Brock Yates, created the world's first broadly interesting and comparatively literate car magazine. David E., as he is known to this day, did such unheard-of things as publishing a cover story that purported to be a "comparison test" of the Ferrari GTO versus the Pontiac GTO. The excuse for the matchup, obviously, was the similar nomenclature. GTO is an acronym that stands for *gran turisimo omologato.* This was intended to mean cars created in very limited numbers for street use and sold to the public to validate— "homologate," in English—a racing version for competition in an important series of European races for GT cars.

The Ferrari was a legitimate GTO, a pure two-seat racing coupe that was also road-legal. Pontiac, however, simply stole the label for a crappy muscle car, which infuriated the stringback-driving-gloves crowd. (Pontiac called another model the Le Mans, after a race they had never entered, much less won. Never mind, it was pronounced Lee Manz by many Pontiac buyers, so the French probably never noticed.)

It was in fact no comparison test at all, since Ferrari had absolutely no intention of lending what was then *the* Italian supercar to a bunch of brutal, hard-driving, smart-ass Manhattan car rats. Pontiac, however, was delighted to deliver to *C/D* a "GTO" that was a heavily massaged, super-tuned, nonstock, one-off version secretly prepared to be tested by *Car and Driver*. That Pontiac, with what was probably 500 V8 horsepower, put down better acceleration numbers than those that Ferrari claimed for the GTO, and since speed in the straight-line quarter-mile was the American paradigm, *C/D* anointed the tinny Wide-Track—basically an economy compact with a huge engine crammed under the hood—as a better car than its Italian counterpart.

The cover illustration for the issue was a painting rather than a photograph, since there was no Ferrari to shoot. It depicted the American muscle car powering past the Italian stallion. It made the magazine's reputation, while shrieks of indignation could be heard from Pebble Beach to the Hamptons.

Not long thereafter, Editor Bob Brown, my immediate predecessor, did a comparison test of the Volkswagen Karmann Ghia versus the Porsche Speedster, both of them four-cylinder, rear-engine German convertibles. The Karmann Ghia, a special-bodied VW Beetle, won, which was somewhat like a Chevy winning over a Cadillac. And then came NASCAR driver Bobby Allison's Joe Sixpack test of the Porsche 911, which he basically thought was a piece of overpriced dreck. Now the shrieks could be heard all the way from Stuttgart.

Brown was constantly at war with "management." The same VP who'd anointed me had earlier that year armed his BMW with an expensive but free-from-the-manufacturer Blaupunkt radio. He demanded that Brown do a "review" of a Blaupunkt. Bob explained that the magazine dealt with cars, not car radios, and then quit.

He was back at work a day or two later, since Brown usually quit once a month, typically on the day that the VPs were provided with an early copy of that month's issue and saw how many advertising bridges Brown had burned by insulting car manufacturers, tire makers, accessory marketers, and just about everybody else in—particularly—the foreign-car business. (*C/D*'s stock in trade was admiration of Detroit iron, which simply was just not *done* in a day when the currency of the realm was that

Jaguars, Mercedes-Benzes, and Porsches were perfect and Ferraris exceeded perfection.)

But one day, Ziff-Davis finally tired of the game and accepted Bob's resignation. Somebody remembered that I, then an editor at *Flying* magazine, down the hall, had owned that old Larry Rivers Aston Martin. That apparently qualified me for the editorship of the world's best car-enthusiast magazine.

It didn't in the eyes of *Car and Driver*'s staff, a group of true car guys (and, occasionally, girls) some of whom drove race cars, had been engineers in Detroit, and had grown up building and rebuilding everything from MGs and Triumphs to Dodge Challengers and homemade kit cars. They took it hard that some prick from "the Ziff-Davis Air Force," as one put it, had been tapped to be their boss. My own insecurity and inability to fire the whole bunch and start over again with hires of my own didn't help. I was sniped at constantly, hard as I tried to be one of the gang.

I wrote the cover blurbs—teasers that appear on a magazine's cover for articles inside—for the very first issue that came out under my management. The car featured on that cover was a sporty import from Ford of Germany that in the U.S. was being sold as the Mercury Capri. On the cover, in bold letters, I labeled it the "Ford Capri," which was like calling a Cadillac deVille a Buick deVille. A number of my staffers and art editors had seen the copy before it was cast in concrete, but not a one pointed out the error. They preferred that it be published that way to embarrass me. Which it was, and did.

The first time the young racers on my staff took me with them to the track at Lime Rock, where *Car and Driver* frequently tested the fastest and sportiest new cars, they sent me off to bumble around the course in one of the magazine's own race cars, a small import four-cylinder sedan that *C/D* ran for the fun of it (and good publicity) in a sports-car class called Showroom Stock. I wailed around the track in second gear, the engine shrieking at the redline as I trundled along at probably 50 mph. Worse yet, I came back into the pits after one lap to report, "Looks like I've got an alternator problem," pointing at a red-lighted symbol on the dash that looked to me like an icon representing an electrical rotor and brushes.

"Your parking brake is on," technical editor Don Sherman inform-
ed me, before falling to the ground racked with laughter. At least Sherman reacted with genuine amusement rather than contempt, for he
was the one *C/D* staffer who from the beginning had essentially said,
"I don't know if I like you, probably not, but you deserve a shot. Let
me know if you need any help." (Thirty years later, Don Sherman, the
smartest Car Guy I know, is still a friend, the only good thing I took
away from my time in the barrel at *Car and Driver.*)

Editor Bob Brown had built *C/D* into a cult of personality. The
testing, racing, car-flogging staffers were all well-known to the magazine's readership through monthly photographs of them everywhere in
the magazine, as well as their opinionated, out-there writing and amply
described personal beliefs. Whether it was editorial associate Judy Hitch-
cock's frequently photographed ample cleavage, Brock Yates's endless
right-wing rants about Birkenstock-shod granolas, or Iowan Patrick
Bedard's dry, just-off-the-farm wit, *C/D*'s readership knew all about it
and either loved or hated the magazine's editors.

I, however, was a nonentity.

Those of us who worked down the hall at *Flying* envied and occasionally resented the *C/D* editors for their national fame. We *Flying* guys
had a good time together and for the most part respected each other and
spent lots of time in each other's company. But judging by the office
parties, sounds of hilarity, and occasional streaker emerging from the *Car
and Driver* offices, those guys were really a hip and cohesive bunch.

How silly. *The New Yorker,* I'm told, has always been a nest of eccen-
trics and egotists who secretly hate each other, and the same, I gradually
learned, was true of *Car and Driver.* The cult of personality was also a
cult of competition. Editors who in one case had grown up a few miles
apart in Iowa loathed each other. Everybody was backstabbing and
posturing, and coteries and cliques competed for attention, assignments,
and money.

One of my first acts at *Car and Driver* was to deliver to Mercedes-
Benz a Ziff-Davis check cut for $45,000, probably equivalent to at least
twice that amount today. It was the wholesale value of a Mercedes 600SE

sedan, at that time their priciest car. *C/D* had borrowed one to test, and a young staff gofer had figured that since he'd washed the car, it was his right to borrow it for the drive home to Connecticut. Late that night, he totaled it in a Mercedes-versus-tree confrontation. Whether he was drunk, stupid, or simply an incompetent I never knew.

Mercedes' crusty PR director, an ex-New York *Herald Tribune* sportswriter named Leo Levine, was secretly amused when I handed him the check, for we'd gotten our comeuppance. At that time—and indeed for years later—*Car and Driver* had a reputation as a destroyer of cars. Some—most particularly the owners of the cars—say the rap was well deserved. Others, familiar with the never-ending battle between skilled engineers trying to create horsepower and equally skilled testers trying to determine whether it really works reliably, disagree.

Though it happened years after I left the magazine, exotic-car builder and consultant engineer Reeves Callaway remains convinced to this day that *C/D*'s editors blew up the engine of one of his $100,000 turbo-charged Callaway Corvettes simply for the fun of it. *C/D*'s editor-in-chief, Csaba Csere, adamantly denies it, maintaining that the engine simply failed because it wasn't up to the task during the magazine's acceleration tests. Callaway has ever since refused to provide the magazine with any test vehicles, but the drama did take place during an era when extreme turbocharging was a frequently mismanaged and misapplied power-producing technology.

But we did break cars. During my tenure, we sent one new Jaguar sedan back to the Jag distributor with a squawk sheet—a list of the failures and glitches we'd experienced during our road test—that was forty items long. And earlier, a Triumph Stag that the magazine tested was returned less one door, which had fallen off.

The most notorious of *C/D*'s crashes, however, was turned into a memorable article in its pages. Writer Charles Fox, a charming Brit, talked himself into the driver's seat of racer Sam Posey's 575-horsepower Lola Can-Am race car, to do an experiential piece on what it felt like to drive one of the fastest sports-racers on the planet. Posey thought what the hell, the national-magazine publicity will be worth it, and if the guy works for the best car book in the country, how bad a driver can he be?

Bad enough to destroy the race car, probably worth a quarter-million 1969 dollars, on his first hot lap around Virginia International Raceway. A photographer caught the car in midair, shedding expensive parts as it barrel-rolled into the trees, and to this day there are motor-sports enthusiasts who remember "the day *Car and Driver* crashed the Lola."

In the early '90s, the magazine briefly revivified its car-crashing chops when a young under-editor destroyed, in a relatively brief period, an $80,000 Acura NSX and a near-priceless Lamborghini Diablo prototype. He performed the latter feat on a racetrack in Italy, at the car's introduction to the motoring press, while dozens of journalists awaited their turns at the wheel. Chrysler at the time owned Lamborghini, and Chrysler's PR director was reportedly so furious that he jumped up and down on his briefcase. The leatherware was the least of his losses, since Chrysler had probably paid at least $1,000,000 for business-class travel to Italy and five-star accommodations for the press, all of which, without a demo vehicle, was now pointless.

I brought to *Car and Driver* neither Fox's élan nor Mandel's chutzpah but a belief in the classic concept of a wall between church and state, between advertising and editorial. I was hardly the first. I was simply following the precepts of good editors everywhere. The magazine's space salesmen or publisher would take me to lunch and try to explain why a great review of the dreadful Renault R5 or the new Chevette shitbox would hit the spot. (Ad strokes were paid a small salary plus substantial commissions they earned on the ad space they sold, so this was a very real appeal for me to not take food out of the mouths of their babies.)

I knew my career as a big-time editor was approaching its end when I wrote a road test of a particularly loathsome, ugly new model from Datsun called the F10, one of the worst Datsuns (now Nissan) ever manufactured. Several *C/D* editors, including me, attended the press introduction of the F10 in Arizona. The others turned to me after driving the car and essentially said, "We need to kill this virus before it spreads. We need to put this misbegotten turd out of its misery before too many people get suckered into buying one. You're the boss, it's up to you to put your head on the block and write the piece."

I did. Whatever I wrote has thankfully faded into the decaying plastic of microfilm at the very occasional library that still provides access to thirty-year-old minor magazines, but at the time, my words made it at least to the corporate suite.

Ziff-Davis had an elegantly waspy but hard-assed Senior Editorial VP, W. Bradford Briggs, who was commonly referred to as the company's token Christian, since virtually every other top exec was Jewish. Briggs called me onto his thick carpet and thundered, "How can you write this and this and this on these pages, while Datsun . . ." wet-fingered flip-flip-flip to a full-spread ad for the F10 in which Datsun described the car in glowing advertising terms . . . "says this and this and this on *these* pages?"

I think we have a duty to our readers to tell them how bad the car really is, I said. "FUCK THE READERS!" Briggs thundered.

Enthusiasts wanted *Boating, Skiing, Car and Driver, Flying,* and *Popular Photography* because they carried hobby information conveniently available nowhere else. They also wanted them for the advertisements, which to many readers were as important as the editorial material. But each magazine's advertising base was severely limited. In our case, car and car-accessory manufacturers loved us because we virtually owned the audience of serious car buffs. Though our readers represented only a tiny portion of the country's car buyers, it was an article of faith that often when nonenthusiasts went shopping for a new car, tire, or set of shock absorbers, they first asked the advice of "that guy in my office who owns an MG and reads car magazines, he must know what's going on."

But media buyers looking for space to place their ads for airlines, perfume, watches, clothes, liquor, vacation travel, and a huge variety of other categories had little regard for what were known in the business as "the pimple books." The dirty little secret was that a substantial portion of the readers of *Car and Driver* and its competitors were car-crazed teenagers or, at best, guys in their twenties for whom luxury meant a beer.

My tenure as editor-without-a-clue lasted just short of two years, until mid-1976. I was booted back down the hall to *Flying* while a new, more management-savvy editor was given my job. The new editor was in fact the original visionary David E. Davis Jr., who returned to the magazine after a sojourn at a big automotive-advertising agency, which certainly stood him in good stead with the Ziff-Davis ad strokes. It quickly became known that ZD had been courting David E. ever since I'd been hired as a temporary stopgap. So much for career-culminating moments.

I returned to my staff spot as *Flying*'s executive editor, where two supremely important things happened. I met the woman I would soon marry—Susan Crandell was *Flying*'s managing editor—and proved to be so recalcitrant an underling that I got fired for good. I look back upon the former as the best thing that ever happened to me, and the latter as the second best. For years, I'd been muttering, "Someday I'm gonna quit and become a freelance writer," but I never would have turned my back on that substantial bi-weekly paycheck. Now I had to.

Chapter Twenty-Three

THE STRIPPER

Most of the work that my Porsche required, I was confident I could do myself. Turning nuts and bolts, replacing pieces and parts, disassembling and reassembling, rewiring and renovating were within my basic-competence envelope. Anybody who can overhaul a lawnmower knows how a car engine works. Anybody who can drive a vacuum cleaner or polish shoes can redo a car interior. Anybody who can read a home-wiring diagram can at least begin to fiddle with a car's electrical system.

But painting . . . painting was a mystery to me. The fact that I could lay down a coat of $2.99 spray-can Rust-o-leum on a piece of lawn furniture did not qualify me as a car painter. As far as I knew, *nobody* painted their own car, unless they were the Dukes of Hazzard. Spray-painting a car was a job that took skill, knowledge, experience, a lot of equipment, and a certain amount of art as well as craft.

So I figured I'd disassemble the car, get it ready to repaint, truck it to a nearby body shop, and pay whatever it cost to have the job done right. After all, what little I knew about auto-body painting involved brightly lit booths with huge ventilating fans and men in space suits wielding spray guns in exact, rapid patterns to lay down a seamless, dripless, runless, perfect coat of some carcinogenic, brain-dissolving, miracle polyurethane. (Remember "This is your brain on drugs?" The frying-egg

TV spot? Breathing modern urethane paint fumes or spray vapor is wicked worse.)

Doing bodywork—repairing and repainting damaged cars, mainly—is a more arcane specialty than you might think if you only judge by the number of dusty little two-bay body shops you'll see in the light-industry area of any town or city. Some of them will do the classic Earl Scheib job, which usually consists of little more than covering with masking tape the headlights, taillights, windows, and door handles and then spraying a coat of color all over the car. It takes an hour, costs $198, and looks fabulous for a week.

Others will charge considerable insurance-subsidized numbers to re-paint a dinged fender and do what seems to be a good job of it. Got it done to our daughter's little Neon after a neighbor backed her big Range Rover into it in our driveway, and the clear-coat finish that the shop ap-plied was soon peeling off like Saran wrap.

Go to one of the truly excellent shops—and I'm not even talking about collector-car boutiques but of the standard high-end repainters who do dinged Mercedes and other lucrative insurance jobs—and you'll pay from $5,000 to $10,000 for a straightforward repainting of a 911, depending on whether you simply want the original color rejuvenated or want an entirely new paint job with every bit of trim first removed, and then the finish "rubbed out" to remove the inevitable microscopic hills and valleys that make the difference between paint that's just shiny and paint that's lustrous and deep.

My car was red—"Guards Red," which I'd always assumed had something to do with the colors of the Queen's Own, a strange choice for a Stuttgart company. (Well, perhaps not so strange; the Windsors *were* originally German.) It is a Porsche color that has become such a cliché it is usually referred to as arrest-me red. (If police radar tags a pod of cars two or three lanes abreast all doing 85, the taupe Taurus, beige Buick, and charcoal Camry will be ignored in favor of the flaming-red Porsche.) A new color was needed.

Metallic silver was the unanimous father/mother/daughter choice. Sophisticated, traditional, tasteful, and way German.

Then for some reason, I decided what the hell, I *will* paint the damn thing myself. I've got a big Sears air compressor, and I can borrow Adirondacker Jim's splendid Binks spray gun.

After all, the people who do bodywork for a living aren't Mensa candidates. If they can do it, so can I. Metallic silver, however, is a color best left to . . . well, to the people who do bodywork for a living, who can spray metal-flake paint so that it doesn't look like every panel is colored a different shade. What I needed was a good, solid, uncomplicated primary color.

Yellow.

I do love yellow. Sunflower yellow, taxicab yellow, egg-yolk yellow, Crayola yellow. When I became the editor of *Car and Driver* and suddenly found myself able to specify the color of my new office's walls, I opted for bright yellow. I spent the next couple of years at my desk feeling like a clerk behind a Hertz counter rather than the head of the world's best car magazine.

But that didn't cure me, and I decided the SC would be yellow. Yellowbird yellow, to be exact—a color that had become firmly interlinked with Porsches when Bavarian tuner Alois Ruf built up a yellow Porsche Turbo that in 1987 became the fastest production road car in the world. (Ruf made so many changes to the engines, suspension, and bodywork—and the paint—of the cars he built that Germany's extremely strict transportation ministry, the TUV, officially considered his company to be a manufacturer of Rufs, not just a modifier of Porsches.)

"The Ferrari F40 had just come out, and the Porsche 959 supercar was out, and *Road & Track* magazine decided they wanted to see which was the world's fastest production car," recalls Ruf Porsche owner Steve Beddor. "And, more important, could it break the 200-mph barrier. Porsche claimed to have done 202 with the 959, so *Road & Track* invited the 959 and a variety of other very fast cars to a test.

"Paul Frere [*Road & Track*'s European editor] knew Ruf and got him an invitation, but it went kind of unnoticed, because no one had a clue that his car posed a threat to the F40 or the 959. They clocked the Ferrari at 194, the 959 at 198, and everybody was disappointed that there wasn't going to be a 200-mph story. So they went through the rest of the cars just to make the motions, and when Phil Hill got into Ruf's Yellowbird, boom: 212. It really shocked them."

Ruf didn't name his car Yellowbird. That he left to a *Road & Track* titles-and-captions writer who apparently liked calypso songs. He decided that the official model designation, Ruf CTR, was too colorless, and when the article appeared, the CTR became the Yellowbird.

Yellow also had a subsidiary advantage: light colors disguise body-panel faults. The reflections off a shiny black car in bright sunlight reveal every microscopic nick, ding, boo-boo, and bit of orange-peel on the metalwork. Shine a spotlight on a gloss-white car and all you'll see is a lump of shiny vanilla, bad bodywork hidden amid an overall confectionery miasma. Yellow is second only to white in its fault-hiding propensities.

I started asking painting advice on Porschephile Web sites. My first mistake was posting a message that included my contemptuous dismissal, "So how hard can it be? After all, morons work in body shops . . ." or something of the sort. I got flamed by a furious auto-body professional who obviously was enormously intelligent and probably just as sophisticated as your typical freelance writer. I was chastened. Fortunately, the guy calmed down and, as is so often the case after such sudden furies, became a helpful e-mail adviser.

I also learned that *lots* of Porsche people paint their own cars. Well, dozens do, and they all seem to enjoy the experience. They paint them in driveways, garages, homemade spray booths, carports, backyards, under tarpaulins, and atop plastic sheeting, and I began to realize that this wasn't a job that required a microchip-manufacturing clean-room facility.

Most paints other than old-fashioned lacquer (which is what they painted cars with in the 1920s and 1930s) require perfect application. What you spray is what you get, and if you shoot a run—a dribble—or trap a fly, you pretty much have to sand it all off and start over again. But I discovered a super-hard German paint, Glasurit System 22, that actually *requires* sandpapering as part of the finishing process, meaning that many of an amateur's mistakes can be corrected as part of the rubbing-out of the paint.

Glasurit is one of the Porsche factory's paint suppliers, and it shows in the price: $558 a gallon for the yolky Ruf yellow I bought, called *blutengelb*—blood yellow. (Blood yellow? What am I missing here?) Admittedly that price includes a gallon of thinner and another gallon of the hardener that gets mixed into the paint before it's sprayed, but for somebody accustomed to $19.95-a-gallon Kmart paint, the bill was a shock.

Many knowledgeable painters suggest leaving a Porsche's primer in place, sanding off or at least prepping only the color coat. They say that what the factory applied as a base is probably better than anything that can later be done even by a pro, and they're probably right. I tried hand-sanding off just the red, but it quickly became apparent that first, it would take forever and second, the nose and left rear fender of my Porsche had already been poorly repainted after a minor accident, and the repair job had created a thick crust of bad bodywork that needed to come off entirely anyway.

So I stripped the entire car to bare metal, which was not that difficult. Paint can be stripped by sandblasting or by serious motorized sanding, but a 1983 911's entire body is made of galvanized steel. Any punishingly mechanical stripping process will quickly remove the thin coating of galvanizing, which is what protects the car from rust. So I used a poisonous, lock-up-your-daughters compound called "aircraft stripper." Not a hooker who takes her clothes off aboard business jets but a gloppy, water-soluble, evil-smelling paste the working ingredient of which is methyl chloride.

Methyl chloride at work makes muriatic acid look drinkable. Brush this stuff onto a fender or door and in half an hour, the paint is the consistency of library paste, ready to be scooped off with a putty knife and then further dismissed with the blast of a garden hose. Interestingly, it works just one layer at a time: it'll take off the color coat but won't touch the primer. Or it'll take off the most recent color coat but not the one it was sprayed onto. You need to reapply the stripper several times, until you get down to naked steel.

I started the process dressed in coveralls and thick rubberized gloves but soon was doing it shirtless and in shorts: it's not that hard to be neat and careful in applying and removing the stuff, though the occasional fire-ant sensation let me know that a drop of the stripper had found its way to my skin and needed to be quickly rinsed off.

It's also important to thoroughly hose off the car, particularly any seams and joints. Fortunately, a totally disassembled 911 is largely devoid of seams and joints, but the tiniest amount of stripper left hiding in a crack will eventually migrate back out through a new paint job. In fact, it's probably not possible to use stripper and a garden hose on anything but a totally disassembled, interior-less, empty shell of a car.

Before long, I was standing on a patch of backyard—I daren't call it lawn any more—that looked like a toxic-waste dump. I'd turned it corrosive with my scraping and rinsing, but my Porsche was as naked as a baby, the color of rough pewter.

Chapter Twenty-Four

MERCHANT MARINER

T here was a time, long ago, when scraping and painting filled my days, because that's most of what a sailor does—chipping, scraping, wire-brushing, and painting the rusty steel of his ship, over and over and over again. By all rights I should be a boater, not a car guy. I should be flaying autumn barnacles off the hull of my teak-decked Hinckley rather than playing with Porsches, for I spent an important part of my formative years as a merchant seaman.

I was nineteen, and it was my father's doing, which I look back on as being akin to me lining up a summer job for my daughter as a waitress at a Nevada whorehouse. *What was he thinking?* Going to sea aboard tramp freighters, in the mid-1950s, was a horribly dangerous, often miserable, chancy, physically demanding occupation. The ships we sailed aboard were elderly and war-weary, and it was a stunningly risky pre-OSHA era. Seamen routinely broke ankles and legs tripping over exposed pipes and gear everywhere on deck and below. They fell through hatches, fell overboard, fell from masts (which still existed and were plenty high enough to kill you, though they held cargo-boom cable-blocks rather than sails). Winch machinery was unguarded, its steam-powered gears and drums deadly. We lived in a world of asbestos pipe insulation inches above our bunks, superheated steam everywhere, and daily infusions of red-lead paint.

Even the innocent things we did had repercussions. On my first voyage, during a hot summer leg through the Caribbean carrying bauxite from Trinidad to an aluminum plant in Québec, I bought into the seafarer's lore that slathering cooking oil all over your body produced a manly tan while you worked on deck shirtless. Fifty years later, I've had three melanomas—killer skin cancers caught early but almost certainly the result of a sunburn so serious that the captain made me go ashore to a doctor when we arrived in Chicoutimi, up the Saguenay River off the St. Lawrence.

I love saying to myself names like that—ports we visited, places we sailed past. Keelung, Kaosiung ("Cow-shung"), Zeebrugge (an accent-twister that properly is gargled something like "See-broyghuh,"), Hoek van Holland, Bill of Portland, Pass Christian, Coos Bay, Callao ("Kigh-yow"), Guayaguayare, Hakodate, Tsushima, Cavite ("Kah-vee-tee"), and dozens of others that will never show up in *Condé Nast Traveler.*

The job paid well. It took several years as a beginning magazine editor before I inched into a five-digit salary and was earning the hourly equivalent of as much money as I had made at sea.

As a seaman, you didn't get weekly paychecks but were "paid off" in full at the end of a voyage. But whenever you arrived at a foreign port and needed money to go ashore—a polite way of saying you needed to go drink, get laid, and buy paintings-on-velvet souvenirs—you could "draw" against not only what you'd already earned but what you'd assumed to be earning until the ship docked back in the U.S. and you were required by union rules to give up your spot to the next guy in line.

You also could draw against your accumulated earnings to buy whatever you needed once a week at the slop chest. (I never understood why it was called that. Perhaps it's better that we leave it unexamined.) Operated by the ship's purser, the slop chest was a floating company store, a little Dutch-doored cabin filled with cigarettes, candy, snacks, soft drinks, toiletries, clothing, writing paper, work gloves, steel-toed boots, and the like. You'd line up in front of the counter and stock up, further depleting your treasury. The inevitable result was that many a seaman paid off after a three-month trip with net-net nothing, largely thanks to R&R in Bangkok, Rotterdam, Inchon, and a variety of other ports that catered to every sailor's every need.

Working as an ordinary seaman—my rank, not a comment on my lot—took me into two war zones (Formosa and Vietnam), several typhoons, one near-shipwreck, and a brief career of working, bunking, drinking, and carousing with the most brutal and amoral men I'll ever know.

That wasn't all bad. They were never brutal to me, for as inconsequential a sailor as I was, I was still a shipmate, and like infantry platoons, NASCAR pit crews, and New York City firemen, shipmates by God worked together and only together. I ended up in some of the meanest bars and whorehouses on earth, but I could always say to myself, "That big Dane oiler is drunk and doesn't like me, but the bo'sun's sitting over there and nobody messes with his deck gang."

Why did my father come up with the idea of me going to sea as a summer job, since I had never done anything more physical than getting my nose very slightly broken playing JV soccer at prep school? Probably for exactly that reason. It was also something he wished he could have done.

In fact he had done it, for exactly one day. In the late 1920s, when it was still possible to go down to the Hoboken docks and just get a job, Dad and his high-school best friend signed on aboard an oil tanker. It was a Hog Islander, I remember him telling me, a simple but effective hauler used during World War I.

The next morning, their first at work on deck, my father's friend reached in the wrong direction while a winch was reeling in a steel cable and in an instant lost his arm, severed between cable and drum by a hawser that bore the weight of the ship against a bit of flesh and a bone. Dad went back to suburban Rutherford, New Jersey, that afternoon, never to go to sea again.

Thirty years later, my father had a friend, a master mariner who worked for a small tramp-shipping company that had its office somewhere in Manhattan, its few ships spread around the globe wherever a cargo called. Capt. Peter van der Linde saw to it that I was made a member of the Seafarer's International Union and that I got a summer job as an ordinary seaman on one of his vessels, a rusty ex–World War II Liberty Ship called the *Penn Trader.*

Liberty ships were jerrybuilt tubs never intended to last for longer than the duration of the war or until they were sunk. In fact, the government felt it had gotten its money's worth if a Liberty made a single cargo-carrying trip across the Atlantic before being torpedoed. The elemental design was based on, of all things, a common British steamer of the late nineteenth century. For a war that lasted 1,340 days, 2,751 Liberties were built—the equivalent of just over two a day.

You couldn't get a job aboard an American merchant ship without being a member of a seaman's union, and you couldn't become a member of a union without having shipped out aboard an American merchant ship. This was a catch-22 that meant the unions were filled with men who'd gotten in through their fathers or brothers or somebody who was owed a favor.

The jobs—posted on a big board at the front of the union hall—also went to the men with the most seniority. Most freighters and tankers were therefore crewed in those days by tough sixty-year-olds, since the American merchant fleet was on its last legs in the late 1950s, and there were few jobs to be had. A nineteen-year-old was a rarity, and I suppose I survived because my shipmates had to know that I was the maritime equivalent of Tony Soprano's nephew.

I'd finished my second year at Harvard when I boarded the *Penn Trader* for the summer in Sydney, Nova Scotia, where she was taking on a cargo of coal. (Not to carry to Newcastle, but close: Rotterdam.) "Whaddya want, kid?" the seaman standing gangway watch said as I climbed the ladder with my new sea bag. I did my cause no good by responding, "I'm comin' aboard this boat." Only a landlubber would call a ship a boat.

Not surprisingly, my name became Harvard. "Hey Harvard, get your ass back to the lazarette and bring me another bucket of red lead!"

A ship's deck crew is divided into three watches, designated by the hours they're on duty—twelve to four, four to eight, and eight to twelve. Each watch has an A.M. and P.M. component, so the twelve-to-four watch standers are on duty from midnight till four A.M., then off duty for eight hours and back on from noon till four in the afternoon. Three seamen and a mate (an officer) are assigned to each watch.

That's why a ship's classic system of timekeeping consists of "bells," as in four bells, six bells, eight bells, and all's well. At the end of the first thirty minutes of a watch—any watch—the ship's bell is rung once. At the end of the first hour, twice, hour and a half three times, and on until "eight bells" signals the end of the four hours and the process starts again.

Most desirable of all is the four-to-eight watch, since you do your duty (alternately steering the ship, standing lookout at the bow, and sitting in the mess hall drinking coffee with canned condensed milk making believe it's cream) from four to eight in the evening. Then you go to sleep—or take a seat in the nonstop poker game that stretches through every voyage—and get up early to go on watch from four to eight in the morning. That leaves you the entire day to "work overtime," for which you're handsomely paid extra to chip rust, paint metal, and tend to other chores. The other two watches both have to devote big chunks of their daytime to watch standing, for which there is no overtime pay.

I was put on the four-to-eight watch. Not because I was Tony's nephew but because Blanco, the deck crew's most senior AB—able-bodied seaman—was a huge, angry psychotic, and nobody else would bunk with him. Somehow, we got along, largely because he took it upon himself to school me in the ways of the merchant marine.

But even back then, my fascination with machinery almost got me in trouble. Blanco, showing me around the Liberty's grimy deck, explained how the big, black, rust-encrusted, steam-powered winches worked—essential engines to power the cables that did all the heavy lifting on deck. "They're beautiful," I said. "I'd love to work on them on my own time, clean them up some."

Blanco erupted in fury. "Don't you even *think* such a thing," he stormed. "What do you think we got a union for? So we can work for free, you idiot?"

Still, I loved to spend time down in a Liberty's engine room, a place of heat and racket and the flailing movement of huge con rods and pistons and a prop shaft as big around as a tree trunk. Virtually every-thing that usually was hidden deep inside an engine was exposed, for Liberty engines had no crankcase. They were an ancient design called a triple-expansion steam engine, with three pistons of descending size. The two boilers produced superheated, high-pressure steam. The first blast went to the biggest of the engine's three cylinders, then as the next dose of steam was admitted, the big cylinder's exhaust went to the mid-dle-size piston and the mid-piston's steam to the smallest of the three. Why I don't know, but I suppose it was simple and economical, as was everything about a Liberty ship.

The engine was as big as a bungalow. Flailing away out in the open, the piston rods and crankshaft spun at a stately 125 rpm or so. Sounds slow, compared to a car's thousands of revs, but when the rods are fifteen feet high and the crankshaft throws turn through six-foot arcs, you don't want to get in the way of them.

Yet there was one sailor on each watch who had the job of doing exactly that. He was the oiler, and he periodically scampered around the engine with an old-fashioned, long-spouted oilcan in his hand, admin-istering doses of lubricant to reciprocating parts as he synchronized his movements with theirs.

The first time I took the helm of the 10,000-ton *Penn Trader,* the captain stared aft, wordlessly, from the bridge wing. He was watching our wake, which snaked like a flung rope as I chased the compass card float-ing in the big brass binnacle in front of the many-spoked oaken wheel. I didn't even know enough to steer by the gyroscopic "compass repeater" that clattered electrically on a stanchion to my left.

After a few minutes, he came to the wheel and asked, "Ever done this before, kid?" Uh, no. He rolled his eyes and called down to the mess hall for Blanco, sitting out the off-duty portion of his watch, to come up and school me. Blanco was neither surprised nor happy.

When I returned to college after that summer stint at sea, everything in Cambridge seemed smaller and slighter to me. I'd spent two months with Real Men, and now I was back among boys. That I was a boy my-self didn't occur to me. I affected bell-bottom dungarees, black turtlenecks, and a pea jacket, and I'm embarrassed to recall there were even times when I wore a knit watch cap cocked over one eye. (Mind you, this was in a day when bell-bottoms weren't yet worn even by folksingers, a day job that the Weavers had only just invented.) I went to Boston bars and picked fights—nobody ever paid much attention—and acted like a jerk. I figured I was just like that hard group I'd secretly admired when I first got to Cambridge: the twenty-five- and twenty-six-year-old freshmen and sophomores who'd come to college late, after fighting in Korea.

After all, I'd even been in on the *Andrea Doria* rescue. Well, not actually *in* on it, but we were one of the ships that raced toward the scene of the collision, off Nantucket, between the Italian luxury liner and the *Stockholm,* in answer to the classic SOS signal. In our case, "racing" meant a flank speed of about 12 mph, roughly the clip of a good marathon runner, so we were late to the party.

But I wanted to go back to sea, and at the end of my junior year did exactly that. Imagining myself a modern-day Richard Henry Dana, I quit Harvard for the merchant marine, if not to spend two years before the mast, at least one. This was 1957, a decade before it became commonplace to interrupt a college education with "a year abroad" or whatever the fancy of the moment was, yet my foresighted Harvard housemaster, the great classicist John Finley, encouraged me to get it out of my system, as long as I intended to come back and finish my senior year.

What had started out as a summer job had gotten a grip on me, though, and there were times when I even considered a career at sea. Considered getting my papers as a junior third mate and even went to the Liberian consulate in New York City one day to see if it could be done sleazily through a flag-of-convenience nation. They laughed at me; it could be done, but not for a total amateur. (Flags of convenience are those of countries such as Liberia and the Bahamas, which have few safety standards governing ships or crews. Declaring Monrovia or Nassau to be a ship's home port, even if it is owned by a company in New York or Savannah, allows it to circumvent expensive U.S. Coast Guard requirements.)

I even imagined someday owning a little two-hatch diesel coaster and plying the South Seas as an owner-captain. This was the kind of thing seamen talked about endlessly, planning every detail of their little imaginary ship, discussing the islands between which they'll run, the cargoes they'd carry, musing about the wahines and whiskey awaiting them. They were like starving trekkers forever planning banquet menus.

My second ship—the first one of my true "year abroad"—eventually took me to Vietnam, by way of Alabama, Louisiana, the Panama Canal, Japan, Formosa, Korea, and the Philippines with cargoes of everything from sulfur to rice. It was a Victory ship—the *Jefferson City Victory*—that in comparison to the Liberties was a greyhound, a 15,000-ton steam-turbine-propelled freighter that could do a little better than 16 knots.

I was too naïve to know how close to harm's way the *Jeff City* brought me. One morning when I was at the wheel—at this point at least a reasonably capable helmsman—we approached the narrow Straits of Hakodate, between the Japanese main islands of Hokkaido and Honshu, creeping along in a dense fog, the captain alternately pacing the bridge from wing to wing and trying to make sense of our primitive radar display. Suddenly the mist briefly broke to reveal an enormous bluff dead ahead, with clear water to starboard. "Come right to three-four-zero degrees," the captain said, and then staggered to the bridge wing to vomit into the misty void. It was the first I'd realized how terrified he'd been.

Later in the voyage, we ran into two typhoons, one after the other, not far from where a particularly terrible typhoon had simply sunk a number of Navy destroyers in 1945 as their task force steamed toward Japan. My only memory of the tempests today is of going out on deck to try to feed an albatross that had taken shelter on the *Jeff City*'s boat deck during one storm, huge outstretched wings, the bird barely able to stand on steel plates. Yet it was far smarter about the weather than I was.

It was a time when a lot of people still thought of Vietnam as French Indochina, when Saigon could still rightfully be called the Paris of the

Orient. It was 1957, barely three years after Dien Bien Phu. As American merchant mariners, we were allowed temporary membership in the Army NCO Club in Saigon, where we went to drink Cokes and eat burgers on what I vaguely remember was a sunny rooftop patio half a dozen stories above Saigon's main avenue. There were 400 U.S. Army advisers in South Vietnam, and of course we hadn't the faintest idea that they were the tiniest van.

My first morning ashore in Saigon, I decided to change some dollars into Vietnamese piastres, which of course was done on the street-corner black market, where the exchange rate was vastly better than the official one. Two Vietnamese boys and I—which, yes, would be a total of three boys—negotiated briefly, my $50 for their fat roll of 100-pee bills, when one looked around and said, "MPs! MPs!" The black market was of course illegal, so they thrust the fat roll into my hand, grabbed my $50 and ran. I didn't see any MPs, but what I eventually did see was that the roll consisted of a single 100-piastre note on the outside and dozens of bills worth about a dime apiece under it. I was as green as a first-time-in-Manhattan tourist playing three-card monte in Harlem.

It was on the Saigon waterfront that I saw a man die for the first time in my young life. We were tied alongside a wharf in Saigon harbor, unloading thousands of tons of mahogany logs that we'd picked up in Manila. Somebody said they were for building South Vietnamese army barracks. The ship was still heavy, and the main deck was low in the water, even with the wharf. I was standing gangway watch, the ramp to shore a simple footbridge across the six feet or so between ship and land.

There was always a crowd of Vietnamese gathered around the gangplank, chattering and joking, trying to sell us souvenirs, liquor, food, their sisters. It was my job to keep them from getting onto the ship. Suddenly a man fell—I don't know why, perhaps he tripped, perhaps was pushed—plunging the twenty feet into the narrow slice of water under the gangway. He bobbed to the surface once, twice as he was slowly swept along with the current. I threw a cork life ring, but it was too late. He was gone.

The captain, who'd seen the whole thing from the bridge wing, was furious. He summoned me for what I was sure would be a tongue-lashing for letting the Vietnamese drown.

No. The tongue-lashing was for wasting a perfectly good life ring.

When earlier in the trip we'd put in at Manila to pick up our cargo of mahogany, I'd gone ashore and telephoned my Harvard classmate Manuel Elizalde, a rich Filipino. He was a passing acquaintance, not a good friend, but I was fascinated by the fact that his family was supposedly unspeakably wealthy. "Hey Manny, guess where I am." I hadn't the faintest idea how rich the Elizaldes in fact were, and when Manny sent his driver down to the docks to pick me up, the chauffeur drove me back to the only house I've ever visited with what was basically a machine-gun nest at the front gate.

The Elizaldes, who were Marcos cronies, owned Manila's prime newspaper *The Manila Times,* the enormous San Miguel brewery, and half a dozen other keystone companies. A dozen years later, Manuel Elizalde, an amateur anthropologist and by then a government minister, went on to earn a measure of fame himself by "discovering" the Tasaday tribe, which may or may not have been the greatest anthropological hoax since Piltdown Man.

Elizalde's claim at the time was that the Tasaday were Stone Age cave people, isolated for 2,000 years in the forests of Mindanao, who still thought they were the only people on earth. There is evidence that Manny had paid a group of local farmers to move into caves, walk around naked, and pretend to be Tasaday, but some still believe that Elizalde was at least partially right. Elizalde fled the Philippines right after the assassination of opposition candidate Ninoy Aquino—the first Marcos man to skip—and died in 1997, so we may never know the truth.

My visit to the Elizaldes was as awkward as you might imagine the sudden appearance halfway around the globe of a passing acquaintance would be. Manny was busy but sent me with one of his brothers to their country club, where I sat poolside for a while in my bell-bottom dungarees and drank rum and Cokes, as out of place as a Tasaday at Neiman-Marcus. Back on the ship, as I changed into my work clothes to go on watch, a brown arm darted through the open porthole and snatched my wristwatch off the bunk. Welcome to Manila.

The *Jefferson City Victory* was, other than a brief hitch on a tired old T2 oil tanker, my only respite from Liberties, and soon I was back aboard one called *Penn Explorer,* another vessel of my father's friend Captain van der Linde's fleet. It would be my last voyage.

The trip had started out as a simple three-week Atlantic round-trip to Belgium and back, carrying coal from Norfolk, Virginia. Before the voyage was over, it took sixty days and was laced with near-catastrophes.

Though the ship was owned by van der Linde's American company, we sailed under the Liberian flag, our putative home port Monrovia. This allowed us not only to forgo those strict U.S. Coast Guard inspections but also to carry as crew a wide variety of inepts—not that I was a master mariner—who each earned about $100 a month, a tenth of what the U.S. maritime unions demanded. As I remember, there were fourteen languages loose on the ship, and some of the officers could barely communicate with each other.

The North Atlantic in the winter is perhaps the most perilous ocean on the planet. The storms can be miserable and constant. The waves are not long Pacific rollers but angry batterers. Ice forms everywhere, and unballasted ships can literally roll over from the weight of ice-encrusted superstructures.

Returning westbound to Virginia, we poked our nose out of the English Channel into storms so severe that we fled for refuge to the idyllic little Cornwall harbor at Torbay and sat it out for a while, a big lump of rusty African iron amid the colorful little fishing boats. When the captain decided we could wait no longer, we sallied forth and were blown like a toy boat into the Bay of Biscay, making more progress sideways to the south than westerly toward Norfolk.

Ramming our way across the Atlantic through constant bad weather and nasty, slapping gray waves, one of our two boilers failed, and we limped toward Bermuda, the only refuge between us and Virginia. But with limited engine power and maneuverability, we didn't dare try to dock at night once we reached Bermuda, so we anchored in protected water at the east end of the island.

Not surprisingly, the tired old anchor winches let go before the night was over, even though the anchor chains had each been secured with a rat's nest of half a dozen hawsers and cables. I was on anchor watch and remember staring in horror—nothing else I could do—as the two chains paid out through the hawsepipes with the roar of a dozen dragons, the friction of the enormous links creating not just sparks in the dark but rivulets of molten iron. When the dim sun finally came up, we were hard aground on a small island off St. George, as embarrassed as a lumpy old dowager caught sunbathing naked.

Bad luck made it my turn at the wheel as we slowly approached the narrow opening between two arms of rocky breakwaters at Hamilton Harbor, in Bermuda. A Bermudan harbor pilot was on the bridge, conning the ship. Pilots, who are familiar with local conditions, guide a ship whenever it's within the confines of a harbor, and they're to be obeyed without question. The ship's captain can ultimately overrule them, but it rarely happens.

"Come left five degrees . . . steady there . . . steady as she goes . . ." he rumbled in his heavy Bermudan accent. As we approached the gap, far below the bridge and barely wider than our beam, the pilot said, "Stop 'er"—a nonstandard command that the mate immediately understood to mean "all engines stop," which is what the bloody pilot *should* have said. The mate pulled the engine telegraph to "stop."

I, however, heard it as "stahb'uh," and damned if that didn't sound to me like Bermudan for "starboard," which is where I began to crank the helm, thinking to myself God knows why, but I'm supposed to do what he says.

Pandemonium erupted on the bridge as everybody realized what Harvard was doing. Somehow, I got the wheel back to center before the rudder bit and we slid through the gap without whacking the hull.

But the hull was junk already, though we didn't yet know it.

Liberty Ships were welded rather than riveted together. It was a lot quicker and cheaper, but it proved to be one of the Liberties' weak points.

A riveted hull had a certain amount of "give," each steel plate working slightly against its neighbor, making the entire ship just a bit flexible. A Liberty, however, was as stiff as a crowbar. When big Atlantic rollers lifted Liberty simultaneously by bow and stern, or a single big one amidships, the ship didn't flex, and eventually it simply cracked. Sometimes the cracks were tiny, sometimes the entire hull split in half in an instant and the ship disappeared in seconds.

After we'd made temporary boiler repairs in Bermuda and headed east again toward Norfolk, I was sitting in another seaman's little cabin aboard the *Penn Explorer*—three men to a room, each called a "fo'csle" even though it was nowhere near the actual forecastle, in the bow. We were drinking something dreadful, some illegal spirits of one sort or another, trying to ward off the cold, when we realized that the deck was working, moving back and forth under our feet. The ship had cracked, and we were sitting on the crack.

The broken hull was the final indignity. The captain radioed for an oceangoing tug to forgodsake come get us. Someone said we'd gotten the last tug available on the East Coast, since there weren't that many seagoing tugs in the first place and there were ships in trouble all over the Atlantic that winter.

It was my last trip. My parents had gone weeks without knowing where my ship was or whether it was even still afloat. I got a job in a gas station and waited out the remaining months until I could return, in September, to Cambridge and finish my final year.

Funny. I was the only pump jockey in Peekskill, New York, who drove a Porsche to work. A well-off college friend had stored his enormously desirable '58 356 Carrera coupe out in the country with me while he went to law school in Manhattan. Back then, nobody knew what a Porsche was, so nobody was the least bit impressed.

Chapter Twenty-Five

"I HOPE GREAT TRAGEDY BEFALLS YOU"

Rebuilding a Porsche 911 engine is neither impossibly complex nor in any way counterintuitive. It can be done by anybody who has the time, tools, compulsiveness, and common sense to do the job in a scrupulously clean, careful, and organized fashion. Literally. Bruce Anderson, a respected Porsche technical expert, gives weekend-long, small-group, hands-on courses at a workshop in suburban San Francisco on how to rebuild Porsche 911 engines and transmissions. He once said to me, "I can teach anybody with a pulse how to do it."

I overhauled the engine of the airplane that I built, and I thereafter flew behind that engine for nine years, day and night, good weather and bad. It ultimately took the airplane all the way to Australia, and the professional pilot who ferried it there later e-mailed me, "It never missed a beat." I'd never overhauled an airplane engine before, but as with the 911, I never doubted that I could do it—with a little guidance, good advice, and the right workshop manuals.

Then I piloted my airplane for the last time. I delivered it to its new owner, a sudden Internet multimillionaire awash in Cisco shares. He lived in Portland, Oregon. I had too casually advertised, "Will deliver," assuming that would mean flying it from its New York base to Connecticut or New Jersey. From my home airport to Portland is just about the longest straight-line trip you can make within the continental U.S. starting from New York. It's a bit farther than from New York to Seattle and something like twenty-five miles less than from New York to San Diego. Will deliver indeed.

I felt I was an adventuresome voyager, particularly while crossing the endless, parched Badlands of South Dakota and then vaulting the Rockies, where at one point, I remember, a lonely, crystal lake only a thousand feet under me belied the fact that the altimeter read nearly 15,000 feet above sea level. I'd flown twin-engine Cessnas, Pipers, and Commanders across the continent many times, but this was the first time I'd done it in a little 180-horsepower single that I'd created with my own hands.

I have a friend, then an Air National Guard senior pilot and now one of Sanford Weill's Citigroup corporate-jet jocks, who had talked about perhaps occasionally borrowing my airplane. Which, of course, he was welcome to do. After all, the man used to land twenty-ton F4 Phantoms on ships in the dark, amid tropical rainstorms, as a reward for having gone to Annapolis and then Pensacola. (There's a reason why Navy pilots are called aviators and we lesser mortals are simply pilots.)

One day, his wife happened to stop at our house to return a borrowed book, and I proudly showed her the Falco's four-cylinder Lycoming eviscerated atop my basement workbench. She feigned interest. And then went straight home and told Jim that he was *not* to fly the airplane of some amateur who dared to dismember his own engine.

"Barbara," he laughed, "every day I fly National Guard jets that are taken apart, repaired, and reassembled by people who are in a hurry, who cut corners, who are working under lousy conditions, and who aren't half as smart as Wilkinson is, and that hasn't ever bothered you a bit."

He had a point, which is that caution, cleanliness, and common sense count for a lot.

Okay. So how do you actually *do* it? How do you ruin—which is essentially what you're doing by taking it apart—a machine that Porsche will charge you $30,000 to replace? How do you do that and then somehow make it good as new again?

You take a deep breath and start. Disassembling the engine is easy: you just undo nuts and bolts in what will quickly become apparent is a logical order. (Starting at the top and working down is a reasonable approach.) A word of advice, though: don't trust to memory when segregating the parts as you disassemble them. Put everything (and its fasteners) into as many separate sandwich baggies as it takes, and it'll take hundreds. Mark each baggie with the name of the part, and if you don't know what it is, just note its location, like "thingie that goes into crankcase near engine serial number," if what you happen to have in your grimy hand is the oil-temperature sensor.

A certain amount of disassembly can be done with the engine on the floor, though that's pretty amateurish. At some point, you'll need an engine stand—something to which the engine can be bolted so that it hangs in space, accessible from the bottom and sides as well as the top. Porsche sells an expensive "stand" that is in fact nothing more than a compact metal framework that bolts to the crankcase and is in turn bolted to a workbench. Which may work in a Porsche dealer's shop that has cast-iron workbenches, but anything that I bolt to my made-from-planks workbench with a 400-pound piece of aluminum cantilevered off it will not only collapse the workbench but the entire barn as well.

So I bought an elemental, rolling engine stand intended for budget-challenged shadetree mechanics repairing American V8s—$40, made in China, painted bright red—and adapted a version of the Porsche holder to its four Chevy-grabbing arms and was in business. I did keep my toes out from under the block while it was on the rig, though.

Another thing you'll need: an air compressor. A compressor is second only to a floor jack as an automotive-shop necessity, and they're not all that expensive—$200 gets you a perfectly good one at Sears, $140 a Chinese copy from Harbor Freight, which imports tools from the Far East cunningly trademarked "Chicago Electric" and "Central Pneumatic." Shades of the perhaps-apocryphal Japanese town that renamed itself Usa, so that it could stamp its products, "Made in USA."

As you get deep enough into the engine to be removing important reciprocating and rotating parts that you'll be re-using—connecting rods, pistons, wrist pins, rocker arms, cams, and the like—number them according to which cylinder or side they came from and whether they were intake or exhaust. Number the cylinder barrels and heads as well, but don't bother numbering the valves, which are going to be reground or replaced anyway. If you buy new parts, number them as well, even if you're simply assigning them permanently to an arbitrary cylinder position. It may be—literally—a mark of anal compulsiveness, but my general rule is that any part that goes back to exactly where it came from will be happy, while any part that finds itself in a new home might take mechanical offense.

Since marker-pen scribbles are too easily wiped away by a variety of solvents, the best way to do this is with an electric scriber or a Dremel tool chucked with a fine grinding point. Scribe the number in a nonfunctional location—under the piston crown rather than on the piston skirt, say.

One other crucial tool that you'll need during all this disassembly is a parts cleaner. I once rebuilt a British Matchless trials motorcycle using the kitchen sink of my rented Philadelphia apartment as a "parts cleaner," but it wasn't a good idea. My landlady saw me off as I moved out several months later by melodramatically yelling, "I hope great tragedy befalls you." It was a bit over the top, but a novel farewell. (Oh, and by the way, Mrs. Anselmi, you'll be delighted to hear that I did get prostate cancer thirty years later, if that's what you had in mind. But I do remain cured.)

A parts cleaner is simply a metal tub full of solvent—choose your poison, biodegradable or carcinogenic, green or clear, deathly effective or soapily helpful—with a small electric pump that recirculates the stuff and pushes it out of a gooseneck sprayer so that you can submerge and scrub-brush squeaky clean even the biggest engine parts. For somebody whose basic concept of engine rebuilding is "Clean it up and put it back together again," a parts cleaner was the altar before which I daily did my mechanical ablutions.

One of the most important things to do to a disassembled 911 engine is to clean out all the oil galleries (passageways) cast and machined into the block and crankshaft. This requires a supply of "shop air"—the efflux of a compressor—and a couple of spray cans of carburetor cleaner. The big main oil gallery runs longitudinally through the right crankcase half and is blocked by hammered-in metal plugs. The plugs need to be removed—a tricky affair—and then replaced with new plugs once the clean-out has been accomplished.

Porsche racers often thread those plug holes and simply screw in small brass plugs, knowing that their engine is likely to experience destructive "events" that will frequently require disassembly and the cleaning of metal shavings out of the oil galleries. Nice thought.

There are also six piston squirters to clean out, little nozzles inside the cylinder spigots in each crankcase half that pump coolant oil onto the underside of the piston each time it happens by. The intuitive thing to do is to spray into the nozzles where they protrude from the block, but that's a fool's errand: there's a check valve inside each nozzle that allows oil (or, in this case, carb cleaner) to flow *out* of the nozzles but not back through them. You need to stick the long plastic extension spout of the spray can as far as possible down into the gallery feeding the nozzle.

All of this lube-system cleaning is especially and enormously important if you are rebuilding an engine that has suffered a mechanical failure, or if the crankshaft was reground. Debris from the failure, or the grinding, can be lurking anywhere in the system. If you don't get rid of it, there's an excellent possibility of a catastrophic bearing failure within minutes of first startup. Instant doorstop.

Chapter Twenty-Six

CRANKY

A 911 crankshaft is a superb piece of work—a tree-stout yet comparatively light, splendidly engineered piece of Germanic artisanry. It is the heart of the engine, and it is enormously strong and durable, a chunk of forged steel that never wears out. When I took my engine apart, the crank had a putative 90,000 miles on it, probably in truth more than that. I put a micrometer on the journals, and there was zero wear: every bearing surface was identical to new-crank dimensions.

The first thing I then did with the crankshaft was a compulsive exercise that I figured would at least be reassuring if not useful. I lightly oiled the bare crank and its new main bearings and put them in place temporarily between the crankcase halves. I then torqued everything together tightly. I wanted to feel what it took to turn the crank by hand, since it was supposed to happily—in the words of the factory manual—"rotate freely."

A lot of fine determinations on a 911 engine can only be done on the basis of educated feel and experience, and this test is one of them. So I figured I might as well start my education. "Rotate freely" means something between having to put a wrench on the crank-pulley nut to turn it and being able to spin it with fingertips on the crank flange. I could turn mine by hand with effort, but I was aware that there was a certain amount of drag that meant everything was tight, with crank-to-bearing clearances that were getting right on down toward molecular.

Literally. Although things such as crankshafts seemingly rotate while held tight by bearings, they're in fact riding on the microscopically thin layer of oil that lives between soft-metal bearing and forged-steel crank. If the oil isn't there and there *is* metal rubbing against metal, that engine is probably about to expire.

So what about the engines you see in those half hour long cable-TV infomercials touting miracle elixirs so smooth you can even run an engine *without* oil once it has been treated with the potion? You saw the guy drain the oil right there on camera, and now the engine is still roaring away. How is that possible?

Simple. First, you buy a $50 junkyard small-block V8 with 250,000 miles on it, so all the clearances between the block and whatever rotates or reciprocates are huge. Clean and paint it so it looks good as new. Put in the best oil you can find—an expensive synthetic such as Mobil 1 or Redline. Run the engine briefly to circulate the oil. Shut it down and immediately drain the oil. As soon as the oil stops gushing out of the drain plug and begins to drip, put the plug back in.

The result is that you'll have an engine that still holds probably a quart of superb oil that, still cold and thick, hasn't yet drained down from the valve covers and other recesses. And everything is so loosy-goosy that the engine will rattle away forever with a quart of synthetic still circulating. The miracle potion that you're trying to sell could simply be kerosene with an aromatic chemical added to make it smell weird, which is exactly what some of those overhaul-in-a-can compounds are.

Cynicism is so out of favor that we numbly accept the idea that some guy with a bolo tie and big hat, working out of a strip mall in Phoenix, can come up with something that Exxon, Mobil, BP, and Shell never thought of, and sell it for $29.95 a pint.

Questioning the value of oil and fuel additives is one of the many things that separate mechanics from handymen.

Another is proper torquing technique.

Torque wrenches come in a variety of ranges—20 to 100 foot-pounds, 40 to 250 foot-pounds, and so forth. Typically, they're most accurate in the middle of their range and least accurate at the extremes, so if most of your torquing is going to be the kind of 80 to 100 foot-pound values typical of engine assembly, you don't want a wrench that reads to 100 or 120 on the high end.

Another thing to know about torque wrenches is that after you're finished using one, always unload it; back it down rather than leaving it at a high setting.

In a multifastener situation such as bolting two crankcase halves together, careful technicians like to torque in steps, in the case of a 911 block 10 foot-pounds first applied to all the throughbolts, then the final 25 foot-pounds. And they do it in a circular/spiral pattern beginning with any one of the center-of-the-block throughbolts and then working out and around from it. Every Porsche technician has his favorite pattern for getting the increasing load distributed evenly and logically, and they all probably work equally well. The only pattern to avoid is a seriously linear one—starting at one end and progressing mindlessly to the other.

Torquing should also be accomplished in a single continuous, even, smooth motion. Avoid situations where when torquing to 45 foot-pounds, say, you get the pressure to 42 foot-pounds, and the wrench is in an awkward enough position that you have to back off and do the last 3 foot-pounds in one last jerk. It's better to re-orient the wrench at 35 foot-pounds or so and swing through the last 10 foot-pounds in one smooth, gentle motion.

Of such compulsive pursuits is the joy of cooking up a 911 engine composed.

Whenever you build an engine, it's important to use "assembly lubricant," which is basically a mixture of a paste of grainy gray molybdenum disulfide (MoS_2) and plain old engine oil. The first few seconds of a brand-new engine's life are enormously stressful, and the assembly lube is equivalent to the spank that starts a baby breathing. Even if you prime the oil system before the first start (which you damn well *better* do), the first few combustion-chamber explosions and reciprocations can be hugely harmful to brand-new metal and bearing surfaces. Ordinary engine oil has a hard time handling the pressure of something like a virgin camshaft lobe scraping past a brand-new valve follower, and in fact there may not be enough oil there during the first few revolutions to do any good anyway. So grease everything up—in moderation—with the MoS_2 mixture, which is almost like a liquid Teflon, and your baby will wail happily.

I took my connecting rods off to be perfectly balanced before bolting them to the crankshaft. Though Hans and Dieter back in Stuttgart might be horrified, the job was done at a grimy, unmarked side-street shop in Newburgh, New York, a depressing little city not far from our home. The dim, oily, low-roofed, machine-tool-filled shop did virtually nothing but build big American V8 engines for local racers.

Until then, I hadn't realized the dimensions of a sport of which Winston Cup, the Indy 500, and big national-championship drag-race meets are only the iceberg's tip. Every Saturday night, there are enough anonymous racers running stock cars, modifieds, dragsters, and sprint cars in Orange County, New York, alone to support this apparently thriving machine shop. Multiply that times the number of rural counties in Iowa, New Hampshire, North Carolina, and everywhere else that Americans adore loud, fast cars and motor sport makes baseball look as exotic as boccie.

Porsche claims that its piston rods were balanced as perfectly as you'd ever need when the factory assembled the original engine—that their technicians carefully chose six rods within a couple of grams of each other. Well, mine were within *nine* grams of each other when opened the block and weighed them, and any good 911 pro will tell you that there were times in the 1970s and 1980s when Porsche, a tiny planet in the automotive solar system that suddenly found itself building more cars than it had ever dreamed of making, was forced to simply grab six of whatever was on the shelf to build the engine for a car that needed to go out the door yesterday.

Does it matter? Probably not. There are those who enjoy the fanati-
cism of perfectly balancing every reciprocating and rotating part of
an engine so that it can spin to enormous speeds without strain, but
after all, those parts are flailing about amid a huge liquid-lubricant bath:
how many grams of oil have micro-momentarily stuck to this piston
or rod rather than that one, and how does that affect the engine's total
balance?

Since I was building a substantially modified engine that I hoped
would be putting out about 270 horsepower and turning a maximum of
7,500 rpm, compared to the stock engine's 180 hp and 6,000 rpm, I
needed the strongest rod bolts I could find—ARPs. They offered yet
another diversion for the torque maven. ARP bolts get torqued not once
but *three* times, to 45 foot-pounds, loosened, retorqued to 45, loosened,
and done up one final time. Why? Because the finely cut threads "wear
in" after the first two torquings, resisting the nut less and thus allowing
the assumedly perfect 45 foot-pounds the last time they're tightened.

Chapter Twenty-Seven

"SILK THREAD IS *VERY* STRONG"

O nce the crankshaft, piston rods, lay shaft (which drives the oil pump), bearing shells, oil seals, camchains, and a variety of small but essential pieces are assembled and laid in place on the right half of the crankcase, which is sitting cantilevered off the engine stand like a big dishpan, it's time for a tricky operation: mating and sealing the two crankcase halves together. Lots of long throughbolts, lots of little nuts and bolts, lots of washers, lots of tiny seals, lots of anxiety. You only have about fifteen minutes to get everything bolted up and tightened down before the gasket sealant hardens.

Obviously, you want to replace with new parts all of the myriad fasteners, gaskets, O-rings, bearings, and whatchamacallits that hold a 911 engine together and keep it oiltight. Well, maybe not oiltight, since Porsche engines sometimes leak worse than a hay-fevered nose, but as dry as possible.

The do-it-yourself rebuilding of 911 engines is so popular that one excellent company specializes in supplying kits of all these pieces, though they also deal heavily with professional rebuilders. Engine Builders Supply, in Reno, Nevada—known among its customers as Engine Builders Surprise, since you're never quite sure what you're getting—will put together a kit of every single replacement part that you'll need to put your engine back together again, customized for exactly your engine and your needs.

They're a reliable, helpful supplier, which is important. There's a lot of junk out there that "fits" 911 engines, but the quality is poor. The crankcase is, for example, sealed with the help of dozens of aluminum crush washers that go under certain nuts. Sounds simple, but there are cheap aluminum washers that don't work very well and more expensive ones that do, and you can't tell the difference by looking at them. You need to trust your supplier.

The art of assembling a 911's crankcase devolves from the fact that a certain sealant needs to be applied to the mating surfaces of its two halves. Those surfaces need to be absolutely true and totally clean, devoid of the slightest hint of old gasket goo or tiny nicks in the metal. And today's sealants are far more complex than the sticky brown Permatex we used to use on flathead Fords.

The two sealants that are currently in favor—and this changes monthly as new developments appear and old ones fall out of favor— are Loctite 574 and Dow Corning RTV 730. The Loctite is an anaerobic sealant: it will sit calmly on the metal in a bead squeezed out of the tube for quite some time, but the instant you mate the two crankcase halves and shut off the compound's air ("anaerobia"), the Loctite will begin to cure—to do exactly what its name implies. Best you finish the bolting, washering, nutting, tightening, and torquing on time, because you're in a fifteen-minute-long race with the Loctite.

The Dow Corning compound, on the other hand, is a room-temperature vulcanizer ("RTV"), meaning that it begins to cure the instant it's out of the tube and senses moisture in the air. It's slower to set up and doesn't care whether the case halves have been fitted together or whether you've taken them apart to try again, but you're committed the instant you open the tube.

It could be worse. An earlier sealant used on 911 engines, Loctite 573, was not only anaerobic but began to set up in the presence of metal as well. The curing process began the instant the 573 hit the crankcase flange and only accelerated when the case halves were mated.

Take your choice. With the Loctite 574, you can take your time laying down the bead precisely on the flange, circling all the throughbolt holes, and getting the two case halves settled together even if something temporarily binds here or there. Choose the Dow Corning goo and you'd better get the bead down rapidly and perfectly, but then you have more time to bolt everything together carefully.

I used Loctite, because sometimes an excess of sealant gets squeezed into the engine. The Loctite dissolves in the hot lubricating oil, while the RTV 730 forms blobs and pellets that can block oil galleries.

The crankcase-mating sequence is one of those things that is simply described as, "Replace left crankcase half" in the factory workshop manual, yet it is fraught with difficulties for the newbie. They range from the possibility of dropping a wayward washer into the case to spending too long searching for the correct socket wrench while the sealant sets up.

If you've never done the job before, do a dry run in advance of actually applying the case-halves sealant. Go through the entire mating/fastening/torquing procedure with a clock running. At best, you'll figure out an ideal way to organize your tools and fasteners to avoid a hysterical last-minute search for a missing throughbolt or a crucial tool. At worst, you'll discover that it's impossible to do the job in fifteen minutes single-handed. I decided that was the case, and buddy Jim the Adirondacker stopped by to lend two more hands.

When I built up my roughly similar airplane engine years ago, Lycoming's case-marrying procedure called for a silk thread to be carefully laid in an unbroken string atop the bead of sealant on the mating flange. Porsche dispenses with such necromancy, but I do remember that I couldn't find pure silk thread anywhere, until finally I discovered a shop that made bridal gowns, across the Hudson in Poughkeepsie. Never mind, if Lycoming said I needed silk thread, I'd by God drive to Poughkeepsie and buy some silk thread.

The ladies in the shop were fascinated to hear that I was using the expensive thread to build an airplane engine, but I don't think they quite understood the crankcase-building procedure. "Oh, that's good," one said. "Silk thread is *very* strong." I think she felt I was wrapping the engine with it, to add strength.

Chapter Twenty-Eight

"IT'LL RIP YOUR LIPS OFF"

I n the Porsche world, p/c doesn't mean politically correct but is short-hand for the piston-and-cylinder unit. Because only 911 engines and some airplane and motorcycle engines were built with freestanding, separate "cylinders." It's the way many engines used to be built but today is a technique reserved for air-cooled engines, since the air has to be able to flow entirely around each cylinder.

In conventional automotive engines, the cylinders are an integral, cast-in-place part of the engine block. They are literally big, cylindrical holes through the block, within which the pistons slide up and down, and they're designed so they are surrounded by a constant flow of coolant liquid. In a 911 engine, each of the six cylinders is an entirely separate, removable/replaceable entity, a be-finned, aluminum-cored pineapple surrounded not by water but by coolant air.

One of the traditional ways to hot-rod a conventional engine is to "bore and stroke it." Sounds slightly pornographic, but it actually means that a machinist bores out the cylinder holes so they're bigger in diameter, and you install a new crankshaft that increases the stroke of each piston, making it travel farther up and down the cylinder. This increases the displacement of the engine, since displacement is a measure of the volume of each cylinder with the piston at the bottom of its travel, times the number of cylinders the engine has.

Ask a typical car owner what "displacement" means—that a Chevy V8 displaces 350 cubic inches or an Audi V6 three liters, say—and they'll tell you, "It's the size of the engine." They know that bigger is usually better in terms of horsepower and worse in terms of miles per gallon of fuel, but that's about it; they don't know whether "the size of the engine" is its weight, bulk, length, or horsepower.

There's an easy way to explain it. Forget about cubic inches, the traditional American way of measuring displacement, because few of us can visualize hundreds of little cubes of inches packed into a cylinder. The metric measurement—liters—works far better because we all know how big a plastic one-liter soft-drink bottle is. Supermarkets are full of them. So if that Audi engine has six cylinders and displaces a total of three liters, do the arithmetic and you'll quickly see that each cylinder, with its piston at bottom dead center, is as big inside as exactly half of one of those Coke bottles.

What you do want to do, if you're in search of power, is to put *bigger* p/c's on the 911 engine you're rebuilding. You can turn a 2.2-liter engine into a 2.5, a 2.7-liter into a 3.0, a 3.0 SC engine like mine into a 3.2 or even an almost 3.4.

This is one reason why Porsches are modern-day hot rods, the upscale equivalent of the Fords and Mopars and Chevys of our youth— the big old V8 engines that traditionally were bored and stroked, ported and polished, blueprinted and balanced, recammed and supercharged, and turned every which way but loose. I suppose they're still out there being massaged by bad boys always in search of more horsepower, but the demands of emissions regulations and noise standards, as well as the complexity of modern fuel-injected, microprocessor-controlled cars, has made what we used to think of as hot-rodding an arcane specialty.

But not in the Porsche world. I remember vividly the moment I decided to become a Porsche hot-rodder. When I delivered my airplane to its new owner in Portland, Oregon, an Internet acquaintance and professional Porsche modifier who I knew only from faceless chats on a Porsche bulletin board came down to the airport to meet me and see my unusual homebuilt, since he, too, was a pilot. A pilot, in fact, who had flown small Cessna O-1 light observation airplanes during the Vietnam War as a FAC (pronounced "Fack") or Forward Air Controller.

Steve Weiner was one of the small group of brave, vulnerable guys who loitered above Vietcong and NVA gun and rocket emplacements and directed the fire of counterbatteries and fighter-bombers against them. The FACs puttered around at 110 mph or so, peering down through the jungle foliage that often was just 100 feet below them. They were easy targets even for a competent bow hunter much less a four-barrel triple-A installation. Weiner's only defense, since his airplane was armed only with target-identifying smoke rockets and the M16 automatic rifle he carried, was that anybody who fired at him immediately revealed his position to the waiting, napalm-laden F-105s. Few VC were dumb enough to do it, but that was small consolation.

As I watched the hangar doors close on my beloved little Falco, I immediately turned my mind to the next project and asked Steve if I should maybe replace with 3.2s the p/c's on the 3.0-liter SC that I was working on, since I was rebuilding the whole engine anyway.

"Go to 3.4," Weiner said. "It'll rip your lips off."

Done and done. Weiner would supply me with a set of six new Mahle 100mm cylinders and pistons and would modify my cylinder heads to accept a second set of spark plugs, as well as polishing and bench-flowing their intake and exhaust ports. (With the 10.5:1 compression ratio I'd be running, twin plugs would be needed to fully ignite the junky, additive-dosed gasoline that comes out of even super-premium nozzles these days.) He'd also bore out the cylinder "spigots" in the crankcase halves to accept the new pistons.

"It's not going to be cheap," he warned me, but having just accepted a near-$100,000 check from the Cisco multimillionaire who'd bought my airplane, I was feeling expansive. There are schlockmeisters who will "overhaul" an entire 911 engine for under $4,000, largely by employing semiskilled labor and recycling used parts, but mine was going to cost more like $15,000, even with me doing all the work that wouldn't be in Weiner's hands.

But Steve hinted at 270, maybe 280 hp out of the finished product, and in a car as light as I could make it by stripping out the air-conditioning and a variety of other nonessentials, that would put it a step above the legendary mid-1970s Turbos, which had 260 hp.

I was one of the first people in the country to drive the original 1976 Porsche Turbo. As the editor of *Car and Driver* at the time, I assigned myself the task of traveling from Manhattan to Porsche-Audi corporate headquarters, then in Englewood, New Jersey, just across the Hudson, to pick up the very first Turbo loose in the country. *C/D* had infinitely more qualified drivers to do that duty, particularly executive editor Patrick Bedard, who twice drove in the Indy 500, and technical editor Don Sherman, a rapscallion Iowan race-car builder and driver who had become my mentor. But in an era of emissions-restricted 160-hp Corvettes, 54-hp MGs, and American sedans that could boast of nothing more than Corinthian leather, I couldn't wait to get into a brute that in fact had about the same horsepower as a current Acura coupe or Chrysler four-door.

Is awesome a word? If so, it could have been coined upon the arrival of the Turbo into the hands of power-starved American enthusiasts. The Turbo was so precedential a car that one wealthy entrepreneur acquaintance flattered me by asking if I thought he should buy several and put them in a warehouse, unused, and sell them in twenty years when they became priceless collectibles. I told him absolutely, yes, there would never again be anything like *The Turbo!*

He bought three, I believe, for what was then a fortune. He dutifully stored them. Twenty years later, my talent as a predictor of automotive trends was in tatters, for Porsche had upped the Turbo's horsepower to as much as 426 in subsequent models and refined the car so extensively that the original '76 Turbo seemed laughably primitive. My acquaintance was left with three old, used, not particularly valuable Porsches that, oddly, had zeroed odometers.

Almost thirty years later, though, I found myself building a Turbo-beater.

Chapter Twenty-Nine

THE AIM AIR FORCE

Steve Weiner, the real deal, flew for the U.S. Air Force. I, the great pretender, flew for the Indians.

What did I know about Native Americans? Nothing, other than what was required to complete *New York Times* crossword puzzles ("Iroquois nation," "Plains tribe," "Oklahoma horsemen"). Tribal names have all those vowels so valuable to crossword writers. Almost as many per word as "architect Saarinen" and "Pennsylvania port"—the irreplaceable Eero and Erie.

Still a bachelor in 1973, I had a cute, twenty-years-younger girlfriend, a senior at the University of Nebraska. I would visit her in Lincoln, halfway across the country from New York, on the excuse of doing "proficiency flying" in whatever airplane was available to me, whether it was Ziff-Davis's twin-engine corporate airplane or a new lightplane that I was flying in order to do the aerial equivalent of a road test for *Flying* magazine.

This time it was a big Cessna Centurion, a five-seat single of prodigious performance and substantial price—in today's dollars easily half a million. From Cessna's Kansas factory to Nebraska was less than 250 miles, a quick scoot for a Centurion.

During the '70s, a lot of us who fancied ourselves enlightened, liberal, and sometimes even make-believe radical did dumb things that we thought were cool at the moment. Often they were stupid things. Sometimes horrible things. People held up banks playing Black Panther. Helped to kill cops because they imagined themselves WASP Robin Hoods. Blew themselves up while ineptly mixing homemade bombs. Lied, cheated, stole, maimed, killed. (I only recently learned that I had lived in the same college dorm, at the same time, as a little-noticed math nerd named Ted Kaczinski.)

When I arrived in Nebraska that weekend, Sara told me that at the university she'd met somebody "really far out" who was involved in something called the American Indian Movement, and I had to meet him, too. He was a minority-students adviser, as I remember. The details have thankfully receded from any imprint beyond that, but I do recall that Sara was one of those people who said things like "far out" and "heavy." Trying to match her stride for stride to appear what we today would call cool, I learned to do so as well. It was a period during which I once used the phrase "dig it" in an aviation-magazine article, totally perplexing an audience of fifty-year-olds, many of whom were wealthy farmers and ranchers. Dig *what,* they wondered.

Sara was a journalism major who wanted to be an investigative reporter, a product of the Woodward-Bernstein Effect, and she thought it would be far out to "cover" for the university paper what the American Indian Movement was at the moment involved in.

What it was involved in would in fact turn into a dangerous, out-of-control, armed confrontation with a variety of FBI agents and state troopers at a desperate little Lakota Sioux village called Wounded Knee, near Rapid City, South Dakota. Wounded Knee resonated with the Sioux because it had a century earlier been the scene of a horrific massacre of Native Americans by vengeful soldiers furious over the defeat of the Seventh Cavalry by Sitting Bull at the Little Big Horn.

On February 27, 1973, an angry group of armed AIM members, many of them Vietnam veterans, claimed Wounded Knee in the name of the Lakota Nation, reportedly at the request of village elders upset by corruption within the tribal government and mistreatment by the Bureau of Indian Affairs. In response, the government blockaded Wounded

Knee with police, Federal agents and National Guard troops to try and starve out the AIM activists, who held on for seventy-one days of daily firefights. Two U.S. marshals were wounded, two AIM members killed, and twelve AIM members simply disappeared while trying to pack in food.

None of that had yet happened but was about to when it was decided that my Cessna—okay, Cessna's Cessna—would be a perfect way to get us to Rapid City, South Dakota, where AIM forces were mustering. Rapid City had a big airport toward which on February 10 I found myself flying with a cargo of four—Sara and her AIM friend and two large, wordless Sioux warriors, Twobirds Arbuckle and Eagle Sheridan, on their way to join the fray. How the Centurion carried all five of us I'll never know, but Twobirds, the smaller of the two Indians, still enormous, sat in the tiny, rearmost fifth seat, a Stetson dead-nuts flat on his head and his knees up near his ears.

When we landed at Rapid City, I was told to stick like Velcro to Arbuckle and Sheridan. Ex-Marines with Vietnam time under their beaded belts, they would be my bodyguards. The danger was not cops or Feds but Sioux tribal-government goons. Literally goons, the acronym for the group's name, Guardians of Our Oglala Nation.

I was suddenly a valuable commodity—an idealistic and assumedly rich white guy with an airplane. It felt . . . well, pretty far out.

At AIM's "command center," a mean house in an Indian slum outside Rapid City, the insurgents discussed ways to make use of me. One bright idea involved renting a crop-dusting airplane, filling its hoppers with house paint, and having me make passes across nearby Mount Rushmore. I would open the spray booms and paint the presidents red. Even I wasn't that dumb.

Well, what the hell, AIM organizer Dennis Banks wanted to go flying with me anyway. Banks was a co-founder of the American Indian Movement and along with Russell Means and Clyde Bellecourt had led its two previous attempts to attract media attention. One was the takeover of Alcatraz Island, in San Francisco Bay, and the demand that such surplus Federal land all be returned to Native American control. The other was "The Trail of Broken Treaties," a cross-country caravan to

Washington, DC, that unfortunately ended not in meetings with congresspeople to discuss the plight of Native Americans but in the angry seizure and brief occupation of the Bureau of Indian Affairs offices.

That cold February afternoon, however, Banks and I and a couple of his lieutenants flew lazy circles low over Rapid City. That was a big mistake, for the foot-high numbers—N22206, according to my old pilot's logbook—of the Cessna's registration were plainly visible. We then reconnoitered several areas that intrigued the AIM war council. AIM supporters were driving toward Wounded Knee from every surrounding state, and Banks wanted to see if there were any highway patrol roadblocks and what routes might bypass them. A buffalo herd was grazing on National Park Service grassland, and Banks was considering "rustling them" to make trouble. In the hills west of Rapid City, we orbited a dam that Banks thought maybe the AIM could blow, to make infinitely more trouble.

Whether Banks was serious or had a vivid imagination, I'll never know. I suspect that he just wanted a free airplane ride and to act like The Guy in Charge. His Indian-brave braggadocio may have been simply posturing, but you could have fooled me. After all, he'd already helped to occupy Alcatraz and the BIA offices, so he was probably capable of anything.

That night, there was a secret rally at a church outside Rapid City. No one was admitted except AIM members, and Sara and I. We were the only whites in sight. The two of us got plenty of crossways looks until Dennis Banks stood up to exhort the crowd but first introduced me as "the AIM Air Force. Don't anybody mess with him. He's with us."

Unfortunately, AIM's membership included at least one FBI informant, who was at the meeting. By the time I got back to New York, a furious Cessna PR department had called my boss, wanting to know what I was doing using their valuable Centurion as the AIM Air Force. It didn't help that in Kansas, Native Americans were regarded by many with about the same degree of sympathy that Bull Conner gave to Alabama civil-rights protesters, and the guy who ran Cessna's airplane press fleet was one of the company's prime rednecks.

The next call came directly to me, from the FBI, since Cessna had gladly provided my name as the pilot. The Feds wanted to talk to me. Would I come up to Sixty-seventh Street to chat with them?

I didn't even know the FBI had an office in Manhattan, imagining that all G-men worked out of some fortlike building in Washington. And I remember thinking how unlikely it was, as I climbed to street level from the subway station, that the FBI should be half a block from Hunter College, on a block aswarm with chattering coeds.

I don't remember what the first question they asked me was, two guys—good cop/bad cop?—across from me in a stark, windowless, institutional-blue interview room. It could well have been, "Do you want some coffee?" but I answered by saying, "I need a lawyer."

OK, fine, interview's over. We'll call you.

They never did.

I have no idea why. Perhaps I slipped through a convenient crack. Maybe the Manhattan Feds were incompetents—dumb cop/dumb cop?—and possibly they were distracted by a far bigger fish that flopped ashore moments after I did. Or somewhere behind a radiator or under an office sofa on Sixty-seventh Street is a missing folder marked "Wilkinson: Get This Asshole."

I had blundered into doing exactly the right thing. Had I told the Feds I'd need to bring a lawyer when they first called, they would have said, "Fine. Lawyer up and then come see us," and everything would have escalated from there. By wasting everybody's time, I managed to derail the FBI's process.

It reminded me of an oft-repeated urban legend—perhaps—about speeding tickets. If you get a ticket, the story goes, plead guilty and pay the fine by mail. But write out a check for exactly $5 more than the fine. In several months, you'll get a refund check for $5 from the DMV. Tear it up.

By failing to cash the check, you'll derail the process that assesses points against your license. You'll be out the fine plus $5, but neither your insurance company nor the licensing authorities will ever know you got the ticket.

Somehow, I had torn up the FBI's check.

My activism was brief and painless—a journey to South Dakota and a weekend of flying, which was always fun, and a single round-trip on the Lexington Avenue Local from my office to the FBI's. Several years later, I spent an awkward lunch with a *real* Native American activist, to whom I was introduced by a filmmaker friend. "Stephan was at Wounded Knee," my friend Dick gushed, somewhat garnishing the truth, "and got in trouble with the FBI because of it."

"Were you indicted?" the man asked.

"Uh, actually . . . no," was all I could answer.

He looked at me contemptuously. I hadn't paid a dime's worth of dues. Lunch was hurried and awkward.

Chapter Thirty

DETONATION

The single most complex modification that I performed on the 911's engine was to twin-plug the cylinder heads—to add a second set of spark plugs to the combustion chambers.

That *I* performed? It was a demanding enough mod for an amateur that it fell to Steve Weiner's Rennsport Systems shop to do.

I carefully boxed and shipped the six heads, looking more like Briggs & Stratton lawnmower parts than worth-their-weight Porsche components, to Weiner in Oregon. Before we were done, the cylinder heads would make four transcontinental trips—a total of 10,000 miles—because Steve's careful work was ruined by air-freight gorillas who tossed around the return-shipment box thoroughly enough to negate a great deal of bubble wrap and newspaper padding. The polished heads arrived in my hands the first time nicked, chipped, and battered from having clattered their way across the country like . . . well, like Briggs & Stratton parts.

Weiner had carefully drilled and tapped the heads to accept the new plugs, since with the 10.5:1 compression ratio I'd be running, detonation would be a danger. (Wait, I'll explain.) He also did a thorough three-angle-cut valve job; fitted new valve guides; installed trick titanium valve retainers for lightness, since the valves would be jumping up and down at a considerably greater rate than stock; and then hand-ported, cleaned up, and bench-flowed each head.

Traditionally, hot-rodders thoroughly polish the intake and exhaust ports of high-performance heads to a mirror finish. But this isn't necessarily what Martha Stewart would call a good thing. A certain amount of surface roughness is necessary to keep the intake charge swirling and mixing. You *don't* want things so sleek in there that the flow goes laminar—a layer of gas here, a layer of air there, all streaming heedlessly toward semi-ignition. You *do,* however, want the insides of the intake and exhaust channels clean enough that there are no steps, ledges, or casting faults to "trip"—disrupt—the flow.

Bench-flowing involves clamping each cylinder head onto a finely calibrated device that measures the volume of air that passes through the intake and exhaust ports at specific pressures, and it takes a great deal of careful handwork with grinders and polishers to ensure that the flow through all of the heads is identical. If it isn't, you'll have one cylinder producing 40 hp and another pounding out 50, to the detriment of balance, smoothness, and the way the world spins around its axis. Why is it called bench-flowing? Beats me. Probably because it's done on a workbench rather than on the car.

Detonation—the sudden, untimed explosion of the fuel charge rather than its smooth, power-productive burning at just the right nanosecond—is what causes the sound generally referred to as "pinging," the metallic tap-tap-tap that an engine under full load sometimes produces. It's not a big deal in a Toyota Corolla when it's the result of having bought a tankful of bad convenience-store gasoline, but in a highly stressed engine, a few seconds of serious detonation can burn a hole right through a piston crown. And you'll never even hear that cautionary tap-tap-tap because the exhaust note of a race-car motor is loud enough to give Keith Richards tinnitus.

Stock 911 engines have domed pistons, huge valves, and offset spark plugs—a true "hemi" configuration, short for hemispherical combustion chamber. Because the valves are as big as possible for the most flow and power, the spark plugs aren't right at the center, between the plugs— there isn't room—but off to one side. In a high-compression modified 911 engine, the dome of the piston essentially blanks off half of the combustion chamber from that offset spark plug, and what then happens is that the fuel charge marooned on the wrong side of the combustion chamber suddenly ignites spontaneously from the heat of the charge already set off by the spark. It's an untimed ignition event, and you might as well take a ball-peen hammer and rap the top of your piston hard. *Really* hard. Locating a second spark plug so that it starts the fire in two separate places prevents this.

Many drivers think that the higher the octane, the more powerful the gasoline: if your Honda Civic is sprightly while burning regular, it'll go like snot with a tankful of premium, right? Big mistake. And it's a mistake made frequently by people who fancy themselves hot-rodders. They prowl airports in search of 100-octane aviation fuel and swear that the avgas turns their small-block Chevys into race cars.

The truth is that the chemical compounds that raise gasoline's octane rating are added simply to delay the onset of detonation. They produce no extra power. If your car never pings with 87-octane in the tank, 93-octane super will do nothing but snatch an extra two dimes per gallon out of your purse.

No, I'm wrong. Gasoline marketers, after all, do advertise that only their super-premium blends contain remarkable additives that will repair broken rings, restore ruined bearings, clean dirty windows, add 20,000 miles to the life of your tires, and get you girls. Caveat, all you emptors.

The trickiest part of installing the new heads was establishing what's called the deck height. If you take off any one 911 cylinder head, you see a superbly flat surface—the "deck" or top of the cylinder barrel—with the dome of the piston snuggled inside it. Slowly turn the crankshaft, and the piston rises and falls. At the top of its travel, which is called top dead center, or TDC, it is almost even with the deck. Deck height is the measurement of the "almost"—the difference between the top of the piston's travel and the top of the cylinder barrel.

In a 911 engine like mine, the crankshaft is flinging six pistons out toward their cylinder heads at a considerable rate, and at the top of their stroke, the pistons, heads, and valves come within a hair's breadth of each other. Okay, a fat hair's breadth. The problem is that in an air-cooled aluminum engine, coefficients of expansion create situations that would never be a problem in a stable, water-cooled, iron-block V8.

Around the periphery of the combustion chamber, the clearances between head and piston are measured in thousandths of an inch. I needed to have .035" to .040" of space left between the outermost edge of each piston and the top surface of the cylinder barrel at top dead center of the piston's stroke. With everything red-hot and running at 7,500 rpm, that safety gap—which might at that point be down to an actual .005"—ensures no metal-to-metal contact yet the ultimate attainable compression.

(It could be worse. In Formula 1 engines, which attain speeds of over 19,000 rpm, titanium connecting rods tangibly stretch from the force of the outbound pistons, and that minute, momentary, but very real lengthening has to be taken into account.)

Why not allow for an even bigger deck-height gap, just to be sure there'll be no contact? Because despite what we've all heard from Chrysler marketers about hemis being so powerful, a hemispherical combustion chamber is actually relatively inefficient, other than the fact that it allows optimum intake and exhaust valve placement at as close to a 45-degree angle from the piston's line of travel as possible. The flame front has a goodly distance to travel in a hemi, and it's hard to get a good, even mixture of the intake charge in the voluminous combustion chamber. So the pistons of a hemi have a "squish zone" around their periphery that is designed to agitate the charge and squirt it toward the spark plug. Too little clearance between squish zone and cylinder head and there's the possibility of metal-to-metal destruction. Too much clearance, however, and the squish effect is weak and ineffectual. You need to be in the narrow sweet spot between too little and too much.

To my horror, I had no sweet spot at all. My pistons measured more like *negative* .035" of deck height: each piston stuck up that much *higher* than the barrel, meaning that it would slam into the cylinder head just before it reached the top of each stroke. What had created this illogical misalignment was a mystery, since all the parts—pistons, cylinders, conrods, and crank—were either original or new and spec'ed out perfectly.

All that Steve Weiner and I could imagine was that at some point during its previous life, my 911 engine had been "decked"—had had its crankcase ground down slightly where the cylinder barrels fitted into it—to increase the stock engine's compression.

One of the unavoidable things about buying a used high-performance car is that you don't know who's messed with it, when they might have done so, and what they did to it. Buy an old Buick and what you see is what you get. Buy a seventeen-year-old Porsche and you might have the automotive equivalent of a former Banger Sister who spent a while as a lap dancer in Vegas before secretly marrying a French cocaine dealer and after three facelifts and failed breast implants ended up waitressing in Ronkonkoma, Long Island. Which happens to be where my 911 came from, in the one phase of its history that I was able to trace.

Weiner's and my solution was inelegant but—so far—effective. At the base of each cylinder barrel, where it mates with the crankcase, a thin, circular copper sealing gasket is fitted. The gaskets are available in several thicknesses that range from . . . well, forget the micrometer and think in terms of as thick as a playing card to the thickness of a Chinese laundry's shirt cardboard. I mixed and matched several gaskets under each cylinder barrel to finally achieve perfect deck heights all around.

Porsche purists are horrified. Porsche purists are a pain in the ass.

Chapter Thirty-One

STOICHIOMETRY

The best thing about carburetors is that you get to use the shiniest, tiniest wrenches in your toolbox. A fine Weber, Zenith, or PMO carburetor is the closest thing to a chronometer, in workmanship and intricacy, that you'll find on a car. It's also the most primitive thing, little different in principal than the devices that laboriously fed combustible mixtures to automobile engines a century ago. Air is sucked into the engine, fuel is sucked into the airstream as the air flows through a venturi—a narrowing of the throat of the intake passage that creates a vacuum in obedience to Monsieur Bernoulli's Principal—and the result is, one hopes, an air–fuel mixture optimized to explode as economically yet powerfully as possible inside the cylinder.

That optimization is defined by my favorite make-them-think-you-know-what-you're-talking-about automotive word: stoichiometric. Stow-eee-chee-yo-metric. A stoichiometric mixture contains the perfect ratio of one part gasoline to 14.7 parts air. Anything less is "lean," anything more is "rich." It's one of those words all engineers know but few casual car enthusiasts do.

On a computer-controlled modern car, the fuel injection delivers a stoichiometric mixture because an oxygen sensor is mounted somewhere on the exhaust manifold so that its zirconium dioxide nose sticks straight into the almost-hottest part of the exhaust stream. The sensor sniffs out the amount of oxygen present in the exhaust and generates a proportionately tiny voltage as a result, which tells the computer exactly how much gasoline to inject.

Carburetors won't listen to O_2 sensors. Being passive, Industrial Revolution objects with almost no moving parts, carburetors couldn't do anything about changing the mixture even if they knew what the O_2 sensors were saying. Carburetors are stupid. The same could be said of people like me who retrofit perfectly good fuel-injection engines with carbondaters.

Which is why there hasn't been a carburetor on a new car sold in the U.S. since the mid-1980s, since they are far emissions-dirtier than is fuel injection. (I always wondered whether the Draconian, super-strict California Air Resources Board adopted the acronym CARB as a kind of bad in-joke or was it simply a benighted coincidence?) A thirty-ish friend of mine, a Lehigh-grad engineer and race-car driver who is a *Car and Driver* editor, was baffled when I told him I was going to put carburetors on the 911. He had never played with a carburetor, and to him, it was as though I'd said I'd decided to revert to acetylene-burning headlamps, solid-rubber tires, and a crank for starting.

In stock form, a 1983 Porsche 911SC is fuel-injected. It had to be to pass 1980s emissions-testing standards. So the SC was equipped with a primitive but clean and relatively effective form of fuel injection called by its maker (Bosch) K-Jetronic—K for the German word *konstant,* meaning, obviously, "constant." The system pumps a constant flow of gasoline that is then metered by a fuel distributor in exact proportions to each of the cylinders in turn, with the excess unused gas routed back to the tank.

The problem, in terms of producing horsepower, is that the K-Jetronic's flow of induction air courses through an octopus of intake manifolding before reaching the injectors and then the combustion chamber. And because K-Jetronic can't deal with resonant pulses of air, mild camshafts that close the valves early and open them late must be used.

How to make an SC engine more powerful? Simple, albeit in some states illegal:

Dump the entire K-Jetronic rig including all the ancillary plumbing and the Stone Age electronics that run it, and substitute two three-barrel carburetors, one atop each bank of cylinders.

Lose the convoluted and untuned stock exhaust system and catalytic converter and replace it with equal-length headers, exactly as Porsche 911s used to have before the era of emissions controls. A company called SSI makes the gold-standard stainless-steel rigs, which include heat exchangers so that you can at least defog your windshield on cold mornings.

Finally, have the camshafts reground to a snappier profile.

Do this and you will have created just about the shortest and most direct course for fuel and air to enter and exit each cylinder. If you were able to peer down through any one of a 911's carburetor throats at a point when both valves were open, you'd see the garage floor. At least you would if the exhaust headers weren't in place, but the headers are a potent part of the power production.

Do this and you will also have created a smog monster, an engine dirty enough to peg any tailpipe-sniffing emissions sensor. Which is exactly what I've done.

How do I rationalize this selfishly antisocial act? I can try, but none of it works very well.

I can argue that every NASCAR Winston Cup race has forty-three 750-horsepower cars with carburetors running around a racetrack at full power for, typically, 400 miles. Let's say they do another 400 miles per race of testing, practice, and qualifying. Do the math: 800 x 43 = 34,400 miles per event for the entire field. Times thirty-three races per season for a grand total of 1,135,200 emissions-filthy, carbureted miles in a single race series alone. I drive my car maybe 2,500 miles a year.

Or I can look at what I do at the helm of my big, emissions-dirty diesel ambulance. It gripes me that we're ordered to leave our ambulances idling all the time they're parked outside the emergency room at our local hospital. I don't know why, maybe somebody is afraid the rigs won't restart. And it's often for half an hour, while the EMTs laboriously complete the triple-copies PCR—the Prehospital Care Report paperwork so necessary to protect us when we're sued for whatever variety of malfeasance some moron who put his hand into a snowblower chute can come up with.

Sometimes there are three or four ambulances idling away outside the ER entrance, and though that's repeated at every hospital in the country, that's only the pinprick tip of the iceberg. Tens of thousands of big-rig diesel trucks idle for hours at truck stops and rest areas from California to Maine to keep the heating or air-conditioning going or to provide the power for the satellite TV in the bunk area. Oh, and I recently read in a car magazine some advice to drag racers competing as "bracket racers," a popular category for everyday road cars. "Leave your car idling all day long when you're at the racetrack," the article said, "so it stays thermally stable."

The poor guy who drives around in a smoke-spewing beater because that's all he can afford has an excuse. I don't. At least not one I'm happy with.

Okay, the hell with it. So I put carburetors, headers, and S-grind camshafts into and onto my 911, and now I'm stuck with them. Carburetors require work. Effort. Involvement. Which, I'd told people, was one reason I'd decided to use them: I wanted to revisit those days when we used to play with our carburetor jets and needle valves, balancing their output with primitive airflow-measurement devices.

The first time I drove the nearly finished 911, the car ran so badly that I was afraid I wouldn't get it back up the driveway hill. It fluttered and banged, and nearly died when I tried to feed it power. Carb tuning was definitely needed.

Tuning the carburetors of a 911 either makes your knees sore or your back ache, depending on your favored position from which to worship at the engine altar—kneeling or stooping. Here's basically how you do it, some time when you have a free afternoon. As you read this, keep in mind the fact that fuel injection *never* needs to be adjusted:

Since both carburetors are activated by a single throttle rod that works a dual linkage, you have to first ensure that the left and right carburetors are working in perfect synchronicity. Disconnect the short ball-jointed rod that links the right-hand carburetor to the big throttle armature that runs across the engine. Adjust each carb's idle-stop screw so it is turned in exactly one-quarter turn after the screw contacts the little pad on the throttle stop. (A strip of thin paper wiggled between screw and stop helps determine the exact point of initial contact.) Repeat for the other carburetor.

Adjust one end of the short throttle-linkage rod so that when you clip the ball joint back onto the right carburetor, that carb's throttle shaft doesn't move so much as a hair in response, and refasten the rod to the throttle shaft.

Gently turn all six of the idle-mixture screws in until each one touches its seat—careful, the seats are soft bronze and can't be replaced, and the pressure of the little spring that tensions each screw makes it difficult to sense this point precisely. Then back them out exactly two complete turns.

Release the six air-screw locknuts, close all six air screws—they're right next to the idle-mixture screws—and secure the locknuts lightly.

Start the engine and warm it up. When it's warm, again remove the short throttle-linkage arm from the right carburetor and turn the idle-stop screws in, alternately one after the other, an eighth of a turn at a time, until the tachometer reads 1,200 rpm.

Now you need a device to measure the amount of air flowing into each carburetor. Back in the days when "sports car" meant MG or Triumph, the tool of choice was the English Uni-Syn, which had a primitive little bubble-level thing that indicated the carburetor's suction level. A better device is the German—what did you expect?—STE Synchrometer, which plugs right into each carburetor throat and indicates the inflow in kilograms of air per hour.

You want both carbs pulling exactly equal vacuum. Determine which carb is sucking less, unless you're fortunate enough to find them in agreement, and gently turn in its idle-stop screw until its STE reading matches that of the high-reading carb. It should take no more than an eighth of a turn or so, unless your carbs are seriously out of whack.

Again, if necessary, adjust the one end of the short ball-jointed rod so that it can be snapped onto the right carburetor's throttle shaft without making it move out of position.

Okay, now you're ready to actually adjust the fuel-air mixture flowing out of the carburetor into the engine during the time when the engine is running on the carburetor's idle jets—the "secondaries," as they're called—which under normal road-going conditions is most of the time.

If you're racing, you're on a track driving with the brakes either just short of wheel lockup or at absolutely full throttle. You're on the "primary" carburetor fuel circuit. You can only adjust that by changing jets. Which is another story, told by reading tea leaves, spark plug colors, throttle-response characteristics, tailpipe dust, and moon phases.

Let's stick to the road for now.

It doesn't matter where you start, but choose a cylinder, any cylinder, to adjust; the compulsives among us fixate on number one. Turn its idle-mixture screw in until the engine rpms slow perceptibly. Now turn it back out again, a half-turn at a time, waiting for the engine to stabilize or respond after each half-turn, until the engine picks up speed again and begins to run normally. Give the screw another quarter-turn out for good measure.

Do that for all six cylinders. On some of them, the adjustment will make the engine bog down smartly and come back up to speed very distinctly. On others, you'll barely be able to sense the difference; it takes a tuned ear.

Once you've got that done—or think you have—it's time to adjust the airscrews. Plop the sychrometer into each of the six carburetor throats and find the one that produces the biggest flow number. It won't be much bigger than any of the others—maybe a kg/hr or two—but there will be one alpha throat. Lock its airscrew closed, because you're finished with it.

On the other five throats, however, turn each airscrew slowly outward until the kg/hr reading equals that of the alpha throat and lock the screw.

That's it.

No, it isn't.

Go back and do the idle-mixture-screw adjusting all over again, cylinder by cylinder. Then check the side-to-side balance again.

There's more—much more—but you get the idea. Some 911 owners get their carburetors tuned so perfectly that they never have to do it again. Others, like me, need to do it every time the weather changes, they buy a tank of newly oxygenated gas, or a microscopic piece of sediment settles against an idle-mixture jet. The stubby screwdriver that I use to reset various carburetor screws is never farther away than is the 911's ignition key.

Chapter Thirty-Two

LIGHT MY FIRE

"**M**y butt was in the seat, and my key was in the ignition. It was time to test the engine," I wrote many pages ago.

So what happened?

It's the big moment, the do-or-die act that reveals whether you knew what you were doing as an engine-builder or should have left the job to the expensive experts. For the experts, it's no big deal. Serious drag racers often rebuild their huge, supercharged, 6,000+-hp V8s twice a day after they blow up or even simply to replace parts that have a 60-second life-span when they're so terminally overstressed. They do it at the dragstrip, out in the open, under a couple of umbrellas and with a tarp on the ground to catch dropped parts. It never occurs to them that the engine might not start or might self-destruct.

It did to me, however.

I had carefully preoiled the engine, motoring it yiyiyiyiyiyi with the sparkplugs out so the engine spun as freely as a coffee grinder and allowed the oil pump to build cold pressure within about a minute of intermittent cranking. That meant the engine's arteries, veins and capillaries were filled with fresh, clean, lawnmower Valvoline. Synthetic $5-a-quart Mobil 1 is my usual oil of choice, but it's *too* effective to use during the initial break-in of a brand-new engine. You want a cheap-o oil that will allow wear to take place quickly where it's needed, mainly between the piston rings and cylinder walls. When knowledgeable pilots break in newly overhauled lightplane engines, they fill the sumps with heavy, single-weight, straight mineral oil—essentially what automobiles used in the 1930s—and fly them hard for about an hour. The rings usually "seat" within minutes.

Back in went the sparkplugs. All 12 of them, since dual ignition meant there were two for each of the six cylinders. My friend Jim, standing by with a fire extinguisher, said, "Go for it."

RrrrRrrrRrrr went the starter, katumpa BANG katumpa BANG katumpa BANG went the engine.

Not a good thing.

I was at least smart enough to immediately know what the problem was, though I'd been dumb enough to cause it in the first place. Six of the 12 spark plugs were firing at entirely the wrong time, setting off their own witless mini-explosions in the cylinders regardless of whether pistons were going up or down, were on an intake, compression, power or exhaust stroke.

The solution was, at least temporarily, simple. I knew that the primary set of plugs was firing correctly, since I'd been able to visually correlate the position of the rotor in the distributor with the rotation of the crankshaft. When piston #1 was at top dead center of its compression stroke—meaning both the intake and exhaust valves were closed and their rocker arms could be wiggled slightly because they were under no load—the rotor pointed straight at plug #1's contactor in the distributor cap.

So I disconnected the lead from the secondary coil to the distributor, disabling the entire second set of plugs. Eureka! The engine cranked, started and ran perfectly, since the second set of sparkplugs wasn't needed for low-speed, unloaded engine runs. I had built my first 911 engine.

A lot of head-scratching and a little fiddling eventually got the second set of plugs on line, and I re-fired the engine for its initial break-in run. This meant 20 minutes at 2,000 rpm, to force all the new parts to bed in and shed their excess metal. And then an oil and filter change, after the equivalent of maybe 10 miles of driving. Why? Because the dozen or so quarts of brand-new oil had been liberally filled with microscopic metal dust. Some of it, in fact, not so microscopic: When I cut open the oil filter and spread the long, pleated paper element out to its full eight-foot length, the folds glistened here and there with tiny metal splinters and shards—silver steel and dull aluminum from a variety of parts, golden bronze from bearings.

Two things that are never done to automobiles but routinely performed during light-airplane maintenance: 1) dissection of the oil filter and 2) spectrometric analysis of the drained oil. The reason for cutting apart the filter is obvious, since that's where the evidence will collect if the engine is beginning to "make metal"—to fail. But oil analysis is even better at predicting disaster. A good oil analyst can look at the data from a teaspoonful of your oil and tell you that a valve guide is thinking of failing, a single piston ring is broken, a rod bearing only has 500 miles left to live or atmospheric dust is sneaking past a neglected air filter. Timing chains, scuffed cylinder walls, tired oil-pump gears, cam lobes and every other part of an engine each give off specific kinds of metal (the signature of ingested dirt is silicon), and the amounts spectrometrically detected can either be normal, cause for concern or catastrophic.

Chapter Thirty-Three

FREE AT LAST

On the first warm, sunny April day, after a miserable winter, literally the first time our woodland plot was free of the lingering, filthy remnants of the deepest snowdrifts, I backed the Porsche out of the barn, fitfully brapping and snorting through its yet-to-be-tuned carburetors. Its tail was aimed downhill straight at a small outcropping of sump-eating rocks. I hoped the brand-new brakes would work as the fat rear tires plopped out past the big sliding doors, off the raised barn floor and onto the ground.

They did, and I cautiously backed and filled till the car was headed toward freedom, away from two years and a month of mechanical surgery and intensive care. The paved driveway was only about 500 feet away.

But how to get the car to it? The soil was soft with thaw and skimmed everywhere with wet, rotten leaves, and the possibility of getting the 911 stuck in the middle of the backyard loomed as the supreme embarrassment. The shortest, most direct route led across a narrow piece of ground that bridged a brook, and I didn't trust it. What if it gave away? I'd never live down the ignominy of having the Porsche winched out of the water by the local tow truck.

The alternative was an end run around the most distant corner of the house, through a gap in the shrubbery that had me carefully measuring the clearance between a small but fender-high boulder and my wife's most recently planted floral shrub. The bush could go, but it wouldn't be pleasant.

We made it with inches to spare. The shrub survived and the lawn suffered a couple of scars from the fat, spinning tires, but the Porsche didn't bog. It did end up as mud-spattered as a farm implement, though. Not entirely inappropriate, since Porsche in the 1950s and 1960s made farm tractors that are today much prized by the zanier crowd of Porsche fanatics. So did Lamborghini, for that matter. And David Brown, who went on to buy Aston Martin. Brown is long gone, but his initials survive to this day as the designator of all postwar Aston Martins, from the sole DB-1 through the newest DB-9s.

It makes perfect sense, in struggling postwar England, Germany, and Italy, for entrepreneurs with a mechanical bent to have turned to the making of agricultural machinery. Lamborghini and Brown only later went on to the manufacture of exotic cars—Porsche did cars and tractors concurrently   and the oft-told story about Ferruchio Lamborghini is that he owned a Ferrari and took it to the factory for some servicing. He was rudely told to take a number and wait his turn, or whatever the Italian equivalent was, and became enraged at the insult. He decided to build a V12-engine sports car that would out-Ferrari Ferrari.

Enzo Ferrari admittedly always had a considerable measure of contempt for the nonracers, some of whom were perhaps even inept drivers, who bought his fast, lovely, but shoddily built production cars. He considered the manufacture of Ferraris for movie stars, industrialists, and rich poseurs to be simply a way to pay the bills amassed by the professional Ferrari grand prix and sports car racing teams.

How dare I say Ferraris were—at least in those days—"shoddily built"? Because I remember the first time I saw an early-1970s Ferrari stripped naked, much of its sculptural aluminum body removed for some major servicing, inside a Ferrari dealership in Greenwich, Connecticut. (I'd been allowed into the automotive equivalent of the model's dressing room only because at the time I was the guy from *Car and Driver*.) I'd been around a lot of light airplanes, and I'd never seen aircraft hand-welding anywhere near as sloppy as what had been done on the Ferrari's tube frame. And that includes the welds on a variety of homebuilt air-craft as well. It was shameful.

In any case, the Lamborghini-versus-Ferrari story is a small urban legend. What in fact happened was that Lamborghini needed to have the clutch replaced in his Ferrari, and far from taking it to the official Ferrari shop, he told his own entirely capable chief tractor mechanic to do the job in the extensively equipped Lamborghini workshop.

The next morning, his mechanic came to Lamborghini's office and placed a nice new clutch assembly on the boss's desk. "This is the clutch for your Ferrari," he said. "It cost us 500,000 lire." He then placed an absolutely identical clutch next to it—same size, same shape, same supplier. "This is the clutch we use in our tractors. It costs 5,000 lire." At that instant, Ferruchio Lamborghini realized the advantages of value-added manufacture, where value is perceived rather than real.

The value of my rebuilt Porsche was also perceived rather than real. I needed to take it out on the road, even if just for a few minutes. I had no license plates, no insurance, no registration, no inspection sticker, no *nada*. I didn't even have my wallet and driver's license in my pocket. But one of the advantages of living way out in the country is a spiderweb of untrafficked, barely paved back roads where the odds of running into a local cop are simply off the charts. And if I did, I figured I'd just wave and floor it.

A week later, after several increasingly casual forays out onto my illegal loop of back roads, I almost ran into the porky town police Caprice cruising past our driveway, probably for the first time in a decade. Fortunately, I was on my way to the post office in a legal car. Had the cop heard that some nightrider in a fly yellow Porsche had been rattling windows? I'll never know. Actually, I thought of pulling up and asking him but decided that was seriously pushing it.

As the Porsche had neared completion, my wife several times said, "Gee, when it's done we can drive up and see Jon, run to Cambridge to check out our daughter, go to the Cape to visit your mother . . ." All those things we'd never bother to do in the Audi wagon but that suddenly sounded like fun road trips. But I'd warned her, "I don't think you'll want to go *anywhere* in this car just for the hell of it." My brief first-day-of-freedom drive told me I was right.

Even at 3,000 rpm—I never got out of second—the 911 bellowed through its SSI headers and gutted Fabspeed muffler. The ride was harsh and jiggly, the bushings all having been changed from compliant rubber to stiff polyurethane. The narrow Recaro sport seat cosseted me like a big palm cupping my butt, and the 911 felt like a race car. I couldn't wait to get license plates on it.

Still, there was something disappointing, something missing, something that made me begin to fear that this exercise had all been a pointless and expensive stupidity. The car didn't *feel* fast, and in fact I'd had trouble getting it back up our long, uphill driveway—had to shift down to first to keep the momentum going.

Oh boy, was I going to have some explaining to do. For two years, I'd been boasting about the "race car" I was building, and what I had created was a loud, uncomfortable, barely driveable yellow elephant.

That would soon change.

When the car emerged from its cocoon, I wrote down a to-do list— all of the last-minute things that needed to be done before putting it on the road. There was basic corner-balancing and initial suspension alignment, so the car at least went down the road in a straight, if not perfect, line. Establishing the ignition timing and doing a basic setup and synchronization of the carburetors. Replacing that bad speedometer sensor. Installing the rear window and hooking up its defroster elements. Fixing the last oil leaks. Replacing the passenger-side seat belt, on which I found a nick in the fabric that would be the start of a rip in a severe impact. (I'd already replaced the driver's belt, which somehow had ripped almost halfway through and must have still seemed satisfactory to the apparently fatalistic previous owner.)

"Fixing the last oil leaks" was the biggest bitch. The leaks all came from the semi-inaccessible thermostatic valve that regulates the oil that is sent to the oil radiator in the right front fender when the oil's temperature reached a certain point. That valve unit was a lousy kludge, situated in a spot in the right rear fenderwell that assured it of a constant rain of road contaminants kicked up by the tire. The thermostat itself was aluminum, and the four compression fittings that locked the oil lines to it were steel—a bad, self-destructive, corrosion-prone combination.

Most people who need to remove one or another oil line from the thermostat strip the aluminum fitting. And they usually need to remove it because one of the expensive bronze lines leading forward to the oil cooler has been crushed by Mr. Goodwrench while trying to jack up the Porsche with a conventional floor jack or lift. I stripped all four of them in the process of rebuilding the entire oil-cooling system.

You can buy an entire new thermostat for $300 or renew the stripped threads by torquing fresh threaded nipples onto the stripped threads, at $30 a fitting, $120 total. I chose the latter course and hoped the nipples wouldn't leak where they mated to the existing thermostat. They didn't, but oil steadily dripped out of all four of the compression fittings that mated with them.

It turns out that these compression fittings need to be near-surgically clean before they're tightened. Even an invisible piece of what one racer friend calls "schmutz" can prevent a seal. And you'll need a dedicated set of four special 911 oil-line wrenches before you should even *think* of dealing with these fittings. These open-end wrenches are specially angled to (barely) work within the tight confines of the fender, and they also have one unobstructed end, so you can slip a piece of pipe over it and create the torque that these fittings require.

Ultimately, it was a month-long process of brief license-plateless test runs, come back to the driveway, see which fittings are still leaking, disassemble, clean, retighten, test run, tighten some more before I finally got the goddamn thermostat dry. I was doing other work at the same time, of course, so it was a matter of using each dash out onto the back roads for carb, ignition, or suspension tuning to also play catch-up with the leaks. But I finally decided that perhaps that was why the Porsche engineers *put* the damn thing in the exposed wheelwell: the only way to make the thermostat entirely oil-tight was to let it corrode into a contiguous lump.

Chapter Thirty-Four

THE MONGOLIAN DAZZLER

T
wo years earlier, when I'd bought the original oily red SC project car, the dealer in the depths of Queens had said, "It's required
that you register the car through me. As a registered dealer, I must
send someone to the Motor Vehicle Bureau and they will pick up your
license plates." No, I said, that wouldn't be necessary. I wouldn't be putting the car on the road for a couple of years anyway, so there was no
need for license plates. He should simply put the car on a truck and ship
it to me. He shrugged and did, glad to be done with it.

I popped the car's certificate of title into our safe-deposit box and
filed the bill of sale among my rapidly growing sheaf of restoration re-
ceipts, but a thought continued to nag at me: when I try to register this
damn car, something is going to go wrong.

Indeed it did. The Motor Vehicle Bureau lady in Newburgh couldn't
have been nicer when I showed up in May of 2001 to get license plates
so I could finally put the incomplete-but-running little coupe on the
road. It was two years and three months after I'd started work on the car.
"*This* looks like it'll be a fun car to have," she said as I proudly showed
her the photos I'd brought along of the restoration process (in case there
was some question about why the car had been off the road for two years).

Check, check, check, check went her red-ink ballpoint on my filled-
in application form. Until the very end—the absolute bottom of the

back of the page. "Uh-oh," she said, "we have a problem. The dealer you bought the car from needs to sign this form."

"Good lord," I said, "I bought the car over two years ago. At best he's a 140-mile round trip away, at worst he's retired or gone out of business. I've spent $70,000 on this project. What do I do if I can't *find* him to sign it?"

Her five-days-a-week life as a fat-fannied bureaucrat behind a window grille was at that moment complete, rewarded as only a functionary's lot can be. She smiled sweetly and said, "You cry."

I hope she's kidding. I fear she's not. But I had a secret weapon.

Thirty years earlier, I had bought a rare and unusual Ducati 350 Desmo racing motorcycle from a dealer in Montreal. Since I was the Ziff-Davis Publishing Company's de facto "corporate pilot," I had the keys to its twin-engine Aero Commander. So I flew the Shrike from New York up to Canada, bought the bike, and loaded it into the leather-lined cabin where billionaire Bill Ziff usually sat.

It was one of those trips that a pilot looks back upon in his old age and thinks, "*How* did I survive?" And there are many of those, when you get old enough and have been stupidly bold enough. I'd taken most of the seats out of the airplane before heading to Canada, and the big, empty, rectangular corporate cabin afforded plenty of room for the bike. My friend Russell Munson, who had done the photographs for Richard Bach's runaway best seller *Jonathan Livingston Seagull,* was my copilot, and he and I tied down the motorcycle as best we could with several lengths of rope attached to whatever seemed at the time to be a substantial mooring but probably wasn't.

Just south of Buffalo, Russ and I ran into an enormous line of thunderstorms. It was ten at night, but the lightning was dazzling. Fortunately, we banked hard left soon enough to avoid flying into them. If we hadn't, the motorcycle would have come loose instantly in the extreme turbulence and pounded the airplane to death from inside. And almost certainly killing a second friend who was sitting trustingly on the floor of the cabin behind the bike engrossed in a paperback.

I flew all the way east to Boston, getting ever farther from New York, before finding an airport that the thunderstorms hadn't yet reached, and landed to refuel. By the time I taxied back out to take off from Logan International, the tower called and, thank you Logan, said, "One-Five Uniform, I think you're gonna be better off holding on that taxiway a while. We've got a humongous line of thunderstorms coming in from the west."

I briefly considered saying, "Negative, give us a right turnout and vectors to the south, we'll be on our way before they're here." It was, after all, two in the morning and I was tired, grumpy, and devoid of judgment. (Nonpilots always assume that control towers and air-traffic controllers "give orders," but they in fact only advise and suggest, and unless it's against the law, the pilot always makes the final decision.)

Fortunately, the first gusts of the approaching storm shook the airplane convincingly enough that I didn't. We spent the next twenty minutes on that taxiway, pointing the airplane into the shifting wind while I throttled the engines to keep it from being blown backward by the lashing rain and wind.

Ultimately, the lithe little silver-lamé motorcycle arrived back at Westchester County Airport accompanied by three supremely tired travelers and very little paperwork. I had a brand-new, exotic, expensive, unregistered, and probably illegal motorcycle and a single scrawled receipt. In French-Canadian.

From the brief period when I was an anthropology major in college, before I changed my nonhonors specialty to Playing with Cars, I knew that explorers working in the Gobi Desert in the 1930s often devised what they called "Mongolian Dazzlers." These were mock documents covered with meaningless imprints, calligraphy, sealing wax, rubber stamps, and ribbons, and they were used to stun various border guards and customs officials into whatever submission was at that moment required.

So I made for my Ducati a Mongolian Dazzler—a typed bill of sale on fancy bond stock, filled with be-it-known's, sworn-before-me's and in-the-year-of-our-Lord's. I covered it with enough rubber stampings to satisfy a French *douanier*. It certainly satisfied Manhattan's dreaded New York Motor Vehicle Bureau office, which briskly issued me a title to the Duck. So I saw Newburgh as no challenge.

I came back to the Newburgh Motor Vehicle Bureau the next Monday and slipped my "signed" form under the wicket. You wanted the dealer to sign this form? Hey, how's this? You like that flourish? Isn't that interesting how he signed his name diagonally across the dotted line rather than upon it, just as he did on the bill of sale? What a guy. With a little practice, anybody can do it.

The Newburgh MVB lady bought it without a second glance. Yet I still wonder. Is that exactly what she'd assumed I'd do but couldn't advise me to? Did she think I was dumb enough to drive down to Queens and find the dealer, or did she figure that a few strokes of a phony felt-tip would adequately satisfy the MVB gods?

I think she knew.

Chapter Thirty-Five

BIG ENOUGH

I need to find out, once and for all, how big it is. Need to see if I measure up to the other guys, if I have what it takes. And to do that, I'll have to hang it out in public, let them size me up, in a very open display of that one quantity most important to the American car guy.

Horsepower.

DeMan Motorsport *(www.demanmotorsport.com)* is one of New York's better Porsche racing shops, a tiny facility behind a high chain-link fence on a side street in Nyack, a Hudson River town best known as the former home of Helen Hayes and the current home of Rosie O'Donnell and lots of cutesy antiques stores. Not much bigger than a tennis court, DeMan Motorsport on a hot Saturday morning is nonetheless jammed with thirty Porsches of every sort waiting for maintenance or modifications, race prep or resale—everything from pleasant little two-liter narrow-body early 911s to battle-scarred, de-caled, waddle-ass track cars.

Dyno Day. The deal is that ten of us, electronic acquaintances from an online Porsche bulletin board, have put up $100 apiece to hire DeMan's dynamometer to plumb the depths of our various Porsches' horsepressures.

A dynamometer is not something you'll come across down at the Toyota dealer's or at the local we-fix-flats garage. It's an expensive device that applies a load to a car's drivetrain (a chassis dynamometer) or to a naked engine in a test cell (yes, an engine dynamometer) in a way that allows the load to be measured and mathematically converted to a horsepower rating.

The classic chassis dyno is a big rotating steel drum, like a huge barrel lying on its side, in a deep pit. The car to be tested is strapped down atop the drum so that its tires can turn it, and the amount of time it takes the car to overcome the drum's inertia and accelerate it to a variety of given speeds can be converted to a horsepower curve. It works reasonably well but isn't particularly good at sensing small variations in engine performance—the inertia of the big drum smoothes out the power curve—and offers too many opportunities for variables, such as how tightly the car is tied down to the dyno.

But if the car isn't snugged down tightly enough, it can slip off the dyno, usually with the tires spinning at a simulated 150. This can launch a 'Vette or a Viper through mechanics, bystanders, shop walls, and occasionally the Wal-Mart next door. Not a pretty sight.

Rick DeMan's dynamometer, however, is entirely different—a compact, portable, made-in-New Zealand, computerized rig called a Dynapack. They go for $56,000 apiece, more for the four-wheel-drive version. "For $100 each, you guys are getting a bargain," DeMan laughs.

Two boxes each about the size of a dorm-room minifridge straddle the car, which has had its drive wheels removed and splined extensions bolted to the hub studs. The splines mate smoothly with receptacles in each of the boxes, called power-absorption units, and the car sits with its rear end suspended in midair, held aloft by the two PAUs.

When the car is accelerated—and we're talkin' footfeed to the floorboard, not some wussy EPA city-driving cycle—the extension shafts spin hydraulic pumps. Depending on the engine's power, an increasing load is applied to the pair of pumps, and by measuring the hydraulic pressure versus rpm, the computer graphs the amount of work being performed. Which is another way of saying horsepower.

But enough of physics class. How they hangin'?

The group waiting with their cars for turns at the dyno ranges from an overweight, greasy-haired kid with more body studs, knobs, and piercings than a used voodoo doll to a perfect post-preppie Porsche owner in Bermudas, a pastel-yellow polo shirt, and stinky sockless shoes.

Oh, good, here's a hold-harmless waiver I'm asked to sign that says if my engine blows up, I won't sue Rick. "The potential risks of running an automobile on a dynamometer have been explained to me . . ." the waiver reads. Well, actually they haven't. What exactly are the risks, I ask DeMan? "If your car is in great shape, there are none," he says. "We're going to load it to the max, at the redline, for six or seven seconds. The biggest risk of all is that you find you're making less horsepower than you thought you were, and now you want to spend lots of money to get more."

Maybe so, but I do notice that we're all asked to stand clear of the shrapnel zone before Rick takes each car through its three runs. "181 . . . 179 . . . 177 . . ." his assistant sings out the horsepower readings from his station at the computer monitor as he watches the power curve trace its arc. It is a very public proclamation of rank and bragging rights.

A chassis dyno reads rear-wheel horsepower. It has to be converted arithmetically to true at-the-flywheel hp. When Chevy advertises that a Z06 Corvette has 405 hp, they're not talking about what ripples the pavement but what comes off the crankshaft. A car loses a little bit of power through every step of the drivetrain—clutch, transmission, drive-shaft, universal joints, differential, axles, CV joints, even the tires.

A front-engine, rear-drive Corvette or Porsche—a 924, 928, 944—wastes fully 25 percent of what the pistons produce before the Pirellis hit the pavement. A rear-engine, rear-drive 911, however, loses only 15 percent, because of its compact power unit. Another bit of evidence that Ferdinand Porsche knew what he was doing when he combined the entire power plant into one compact unit.

I'm scheduled to run last, and I'm hoping everybody else will have gone home by then. No such luck. People crowd around to peer at the funny-looking things on top of the engine. "Carburetors," I tell them. DeMan climbs in and asks what the redline is. "Seventy-five hundred," I say, which is 1,000 turns higher than a stock 911, "but I've never taken it that high." Rick decides 7,200 will be plenty.

It's over in a minute. Clutch out, the engine bogs briefly as the dyno's hydraulic pump loads it up, and then three times the little Porsche screams to peak. Nothing blows up. 232.7, 233, 234.6 . . . Good lord, I'm putting out 276 hp at the flywheel, after adding the requisite 15 percent. That's six better than my fondest hope, and the graphs that DeMan prints out show that with some adroit tuning and rejetting, there's yet more horsepower lurking under the Porsche's little engine hatch.

It may not be much compared to 500-hp Vipers and 400-hp SVT Mustangs, but for a twenty-year-old, 2,500-pound car, it's plenty. I drive home happy in the knowledge that I'm Big Enough.

Big enough? One thing about horsepower, I quickly realize, is that such words as "plenty" and "enough" don't apply. The operative term is "most." A quick fax to California and I have a selection of different carburetor jets, emulsion tubes, and air jets and am back on DeMan's doorstep with an appointment for a private dyno session. His experienced hands will be on the carbs and the distributor timing for a serious tuning session.

"You're running so rich you ought to be a Superfund Site," he quickly concludes, his eyes watering from the noxious fumes. Three hours and $654.91 later—plus $150 for the extra tryout carburetor parts I bought—DeMan is done. With the carbs and timing set for optimum horsepower and torque, my little yellow project car is cranking out 290 hp and 288 foot-pounds of table-flat torque curve. Now I'm happy.

Chapter Thirty-Six

FORTY GOOD YEARS

When my 911SC was shipped from Stuttgart in 1983, it was intended to be among the last of a dying breed. Porsche's engineers were through with this odd rear-engine, air/oil-cooled, 2 | 2 configuration with backseats usable only by individuals whose ages didn't exceed their hat sizes. Still, the 911 had had a good run—exactly twenty years, by the time mine was made—and the company had already named its successor.

That young prince was a far more modern, more luxurious, more conventional yet dramatic sports car, called the Porsche 928. Its engine, a complex and charismatic V8 of considerable power, was in front of the driver, and it was liquid-cooled. Good riddance to the aging 911 and its threshing-machine flat six that was kept from melting by an air blast from a fan.

Not so fast.

In 2003—another twenty years on—the Porsche 911 configuration celebrated its fortieth anniversary, while the 928 had been resting in its automotive grave for a dozen years. Used Porsche 928s—once-awesome, luxurious, 165-mph grand touring cars—can today be bought for a variety of songs, since their four-cam, 32-valve engines are so expensive to repair or overhaul that it's often not worth the effort.

Yet the little 911 is forty-plus, and I'd be willing to bet that the evergreen model will celebrate a fiftieth, and when it does, the 911 will in 2013 be more successful and more lusted after than ever.

Farther than that I won't go. John McPhee wrote that "[*New Yorker* Editor] William Shawn . . . used to tell his nonfiction writers that the world's worst subject was the future, [which] could too easily come loose and take off on unexpected vectors." McPhee did add that, "Reacting to a proposal of mine, he once slightly modified his position, inform-ing me that the future was actually the second-worst subject in the world, the worst being the Loch Ness monster."

The 928 was a stunning car, faster, more powerful, and more expen-sive than the equivalent 911, but it indeed took off on unexpected vec-tors. I remember doing an indicated 168 mph in a 928 S4 on a long, straight, empty two-lane in the desert country of eastern Oregon in 1987, at a time when 911s were barely capable of 150. Porsche had placed the bulbous but smoothly delineated 928 at the top of the prod-uct line. To aspire to a 928 was to aspire to the best that Porsche had to offer, the company said. The 928 was the car that Tom Cruise let roll into the lake in his first big film, *Risky Business,* a piece of product placement that hinted at the hopes Porsche had for the car.

Fortunately, hard-core Porsche buyers refused to fall for it.

Every once in a while, a market for a product reacts in a way that none of the smart guys ever predicted. Certainly there are products, such as the Cadillac DeVille and just about every Buick ever made, that temporarily retain a faithful audience, which grows a year older every 365 days, and eventually both product and market die, but the 911 ex-perience reminds me of what happened to Cessna, the world's biggest light-airplane manufacturer, in the late 1960s.

Cessna had for decades been making a single-engine, four-seat lightplane called the 172, familiarly known as the Cessna Skyhawk. More a Skyhen, the 172 was a plodder, an awkward-looking, poultry-chested but productive domestic bird that sold by the thousands (huge numbers in the rarefied stratum of personal airplanes). It was the safest, easiest-to-fly airplane ever manufactured.

But Cessna engineers and marketers had a better idea. The Sky-hawk design dated back to 1955. Its wings were held on by thick aluminum struts, just like those on the *Spirit of St. Louis.* It was slow, cruising at 125 mph, about what a Porsche 911 driver did on the auto-bahn if there was no hurry. It had long ago earned a reputation as the Buick of lightplanes—a stodgy airplane that handled like a Buick but that could be safely operated by even aviation novitiates.

So what did Cessna do? They introduced the Cardinal, a four-seat single intended to put the Skyhawk out of business. The Cardinal was quite beautiful, with tapered cantilever wings (no struts); a modern one-piece stabilator in place of a conventional horizontal tail, just as most jet fighters have; and a sleek, forward-thrusting windshield and cowl rather than the Skyhawk's loaf-of-bread nose.

Just like the Porsche 928, the Cardinal went faster, cost more, and was a substantial step into the future. But it lasted only eleven years before minuscule sales put it out of production. The Cessna 172 Sky-hawk, however, a forty-nine-year-old design, continues to be manufac-tured in the twenty-first century, still the safest, most economical, and in many ways the pleasantest four-place lightplane ever built. People who appreciate a product for its veritable virtues sometimes under-stand things the marketers don't.

Perhaps my twenty-year-old 911 is the Cessna Skyhawk of auto-mobiles. High-performance Porsche fans will be horrified by the meta-phor, since the 'Hawk is a stodgy old bird. But like that Cessna, the midlife 911 is a flawed but successful design, doing exactly what its designers set out to accomplish in the early 1960s—providing sporty, predictable performance with the utmost in durability, economy, and reliability.

I have a friend who does public-relations work for Porsche in the U.S. It was once his lot to accompany Ferry Porsche (company founder Ferdinand's son and at that point chairman of the board) to a Porsche Parade, which is what the Porsche Club of America calls its sub-stantial yearly convention. The prime feature of each PCA Parade is a *concours d'elegance,* at which the most perfect, most spectacular, most anally restored and maintained Porsches in a variety of categories are awarded prizes. Rumor has it that at one Parade, the grand prize went to a Porsche owner who bought a brand-new 911, disassembled it, perfectly repainted or replated every visible part and reassembled a car that was quite literally better than new.

"This must make you proud," my friend said to Ferry Porsche as they surveyed a field filled with cars awaiting judgment, their owners frantically cleaning the insides of exhaust pipes, detailing nooks and crannies with Q-tips, siliconing ignition wires, polishing tires and ensuring that the hidden undersides of their cars were cleaner than a kitchen counter. "Six hundred beautiful cars, each with your family's name on it."

"It makes me sad," Ferry said. "Our cars were meant to be driven, not polished."

Today, I have a car that is meant to be driven, not polished, and Ferry would love it. Sure, it has faults. No paint job done as amateurishly as mine is perfect, but only I know where the few dribbles and runs are. The dashboard overlay is cracked just below the radio, there's a little trim adhesive showing on the driver's-side door, I have yet to figure out how to hook up the rear-window defroster wires, and I could have done a lot better job of painting the inside of the trunk, even though the spray-can silver is entirely hidden by carpeting.

But I tell people, "Hey, it's a utility car, not a museum piece. A driver, not a garage queen." TV talk-show host Jay Leno, a serious classic-car collector, would understand. A truly perfect restoration of something like a Duesenberg or a Hispano-Suiza would score 100 points at a major *concours,* and Leno once said, "You restore 'em to 100 points, and then you drive 'em back down to 80." If you can't drive a car, what's the point?

And I did it all myself, other than for the specialized machine-shop work that was needed. I don't mind a bit taking self-satisfied pride in that, for it was the essence of the exercise. We're a society of increasingly sedentary folk who know less and less about how to wire a table lamp, repair a leaky dishwasher, replace a clothes-dryer drive belt, fix the flat tire on our kid's bike or plug a new PCI card into a computer. I don't ever want to be one of those helpless innocents.

The little yellow 911 also provides me with pleasures that no modern machine can as easily afford. Like every Porsche ever made, it can be used as a race car, and daughter Brook and I indeed presume to "race" it. The word has to be in quotes because *real* racing involves direct competition between cars vastly better prepared and far more highly modified than mine. We simply go out on racetracks, when allowed, and drive fast without any thought of beating anyone.

The little yellow 911 is a *poseur,* really, even with its wide-belted Simpson five-point harness, big black 303 numbers, dinner-plate-size Momo competition wheel, hip-hugging Recaro track seats, fat-tubed roll bar, fire extinguisher, and a huge red loss-of-oil-pressure LED light in place of the clock on the dashboard. Wow, just like a real race car! Yet anybody who drives a real race car will be as amused by my pretension as I am by people who restore cars by writing checks instead of turning wrenches. When other drivers at the track ask my daughter who built her car, she says, "My Dad." No, they say, not who bought it, who *built* it. "My Dad."

There are few other automobiles made—Ferraris quickly come to mind—that can be taken directly from driveway to racetrack and run as fast as they can go with no fear of mechanical failure. After half a century of playing with cars, I finally have one I truly *can* play with. And if I'm too old to appreciate it, my little girl can always take the wheel.

I'm upside-down, underwater, and in over my head—three phrases equally favored among car restorers who have a more investment-minded view of the trade. But every time I pull my little yellow car out of its tarpaulin tent—no, we don't even have a garage, out here in the woods—and go for a pointless drive, I'm renewed again. If there's a better reason for taking two years to sink a small fortune into a used car, I don't know it.